Sacred Vision:
A Man's Legacy

SACRED VISION:
A MAN'S LEGACY

David C. James

Forward by
Alan Jones, Dean of Grace Cathedral, San Francisco

Authors Choice Press
San Jose New York Lincoln Shanghai

Sacred Vision: A Man's Legacy

Authors Choice Press
an imprint of iUniverse.com, Inc.

For information address:
iUniverse.com, Inc.
620 North 48th Street, Suite 201
Lincoln, NE 68504-3467
www.iuniverse.com

ISBN: 0-595-13959-0

Printed in the United States of America

Advance Praise for
Sacred Vision: A Man's Legacy

"This is a handbook for both men and women on being human. David James helps us—with doses of sanity, human, and confrontation—to recover the vision of our sacred role as responsible and joyful leaders in the human family. This book is rather like an encouraging letter from an older and wiser brother who, having made his own mistakes and messes, wants to support us all."

Alan Jones
Dean of Grace Cathedral in San Francisco
Author of "The Soul's Journey," "Sacrifice and Delight,"
"Soul Making," and Passion for Pilgrimage

"This is not like any other book for men that you'll find on the market today! David James digs deep into a man's soul and we come out stronger for it. In general, males prefer victor/defeated kinds of stories. They like to be winners and not losers—which puts them at a serious disadvantage in ever understanding the teaching of most spiritual masters. David James is lining us up with the truly great—and always subversive—wisdom of the ages in this book. Read this—and "ruin" your whole life!"

Richard Rohr, OFM
The Center of Action and Contemplation in Albuquerque, NM.
Author of "The Wild Man's Journey," "Quest for the Grail" and
"Job and the Meaning of Suffering."

"David James' book, Sacred Vision, will surprise you…perhaps on every page. Whether you choose to read one of these brief selections daily, or sample several at one sitting, you will discover that Fr. James has blended wisdom from psychology, scripture, and life in every segment. Suddenly, you'll realize how sacred vision is created—from a soul's journey into a man's own depths in dialogue with faith and the wisdom of many voices.

Dwight Judy, Ph.D.
Director of the Oakwood Spiritual Life Institute, Syracuse, IN.
Author of "Healing the Male Soul: Christianity and the Mythic Journey,"
Embracing God: Praying with Teresa of Avila;
and "Christian Meditation and Inner Healing"

Dedicated to my father,

Donald P. James

Who, when Police Officers only made $400.00 a month,
worked on patrol all night and then
drove a dump truck all day
so we would have food and clothing.

Your Legacy Will Live On

In Memory of

Joseph Cardinal Bernadin

1928–1997

*A Legacy Maker who showed us
how to build common ground.*

Acknowledgments

Special thanks go to the following for their help in this writing project:

*Alan Jones, Dean of Grace Cathedral in San Francisco
for his encouragement and inspiring Forward.*

Richard Rohr, OFM for his suggestions and review.

*Jim Clarke, of the Catholic Archdiocese of Los Angeles and Bishop Jon
Bruno of the Episcopal Diocese of Los Angeles…co-laborers in the Gospel.*

*To my students at Trinity College of Graduate Studies in Anaheim for their
helpful feedback and challenges.*

*To all the men at my talks and retreats who have shared their hearts in a
way that is vulnerable and full of integrity.*

*To the People of St. Mark's Episcopal Church in Tracy who have opened
their hearts and their homes to us.*

*To Don Pattison at Pomona College & Joe Bierek at St. Francis, La
Quinta for editorial review & suggestions.*

*And last, but certainly not least, to my wife Audrey who has filled my
heart with love, tenderness and compassion.*

There was a scholar of the law who stood up to test him and said,
"Teacher, what must I do to inherit eternal life?" Jesus said to him,
"What is written in the law? How do you read it?"
He said in reply, "You shall love the Lord, your God, with all your
heart, with all your being, with all your strength, and with all your
mind, and your neighbor as yourself."

"Yes!" He replied to him, "Do this and you'll really live."

A paraphrase of Luke 10: 25-28

"I don't know what your destiny will be, but one thing I know:
the only ones among you who will be truly happy
are those who will have sought and found how to serve."

Albert Schweitzer

Contents

Foreword

by Alan Jones

America is, in many way a joyless polity—at least it seems so to many outside American culture. When things are going well we worry! We have the same things to worry about—terrorism, global warming, the international recession—as everybody else, but we also have a rich selection of the pathologies of affluence, from drug-taking to excessive litigation, from family breakdown to the militia movement, from clinical depression to social breakdown. If you're a man who is awake and aware, you have one more thing to keep you awake at night. How to be truly a man in the middle of the chaos. It's not a trivial question but it can become obsessive, tragic and sometimes hilarious. There are many sicknesses in the world and, since it is a human trait to look for scapegoats, men come in handy, under the blanket term of Patriarchy, to be the focus of blame for many of the world's ills. There's some truth in this but when it becomes the whole truth, pursuit of Truth with a capital "T" can be in the service of a great lie. Father David James is a truth-teller and, therefore, a man who has a sense of proportion and balance—qualities not always easy to find in discussions about men. When I think of many of the fine men I know—especially hard-workers who enjoy some measure of worldly success—several things come to mind: work as a compulsion, money as a place of safety, intimate relations as first a refuge then a suffocating trap. How does one begin to address the complexities of modern life as it presses in upon all of us—men in particular?

David starts off with a startling assertion which the reader may miss if he's not careful. (I am assuming that most of his readers will be men, although I hope many women will read and be fed by this book, because it is, in many ways, a hand-book for being human). The startling and encouraging claim—namely: the sacredness of our identity is a gift. It is a holy, awesome, and wonderful thing to be called to be human. Being human is both a given and gift. We were made for wonder, passion, generosity, thankfulness. This is the place to start.

When Helen Keller was asked if there was anything worse than being blind—"Yes, Having no vision!" Perhaps it was ever thus, but there is some truth to our having the end-of-the-millennium jitters about the fate of the human project. There are various models of what it is to be human vying for our attention: consumer; rugged individualist, alienated wanderer. One of the ironies is that we in the affluent West are often infected with the mentality of scarcity which not only makes us ungenerous but impoverishes the imagination as well. Men, at least in the West, are also under attack. According the one scenario, we are insensitive, power-driven, unconscious, aggressive, irresponsible and silly school boys—sexually immature at best, predators at worst. The question of what it means to be a man is, to say the least, problematic! It's as if we have lost whole octaves of passion (to use a phrase of John Updike) and suffered deep wounds in our sexuality and masculinity. David James helps us—with doses of sanity, humor, and confrontation—to recover the vision of our sacred role as responsible and joyful leaders in the human family. Trying to understand what it means to be a man or a woman today requires a special wisdom, even a kind of cunning, because of the traps set in our path—for example, the temptation to lazy thinking which condemns or praises indiscriminately. Whatever our status—married or single, straight or gay, alone or in a committed relationship—we are called to protect and celebrate the bonds of the human family. All of us have a special responsibility to pass on the sacred vision of human identity to children—not only our own but all children.

How does one find and embrace a vision of life which is true and sustaining in a world where old boundaries seem to be breaking down? When we wake up to our sacred identity we realize that we are called into a community of trust in which the members of the Human Family experience a powerful sense of possibility and confidence about the future. The challenge is to find rules for living which are liberating rather than repressive, that lead to joy rather than despair. The last thing men need today is a rule book with which to beat up on themselves. I don't need scolding so that I close down as I try to shield myself from disappointments and thwarted aspirations. We will make mistakes. Occasionally we will betray the best that is in us. Ben Zander, the conductor of the Boston Philharmonic, tells his students to raise up the arms in wonder and shout "How fascinating!" whenever they make a mistake! He insists that each mistake we make is a basis for learning. Each failure to love can either reinforce our self-rejection or be a doorway to new depths of loving.

My friend, Richard Pascale, one of the best teachers I know in helping business leaders grow into spiritual maturity writes that there are four key indicators for enterprises which not only survive but flourish in a chaotic and ever-changing environment. What he writes about the world of business applies to our personal lives—especially to men. Our true flourishing requires our sharing power and enlarging our vision in an open community, with a willingness to embrace the new. In these meditations with their probing questions, David James address these four basic issues of human flourishing. How can we be both properly powerful and genuinely gentle? Men (women too, of course) struggle with issue of power. How often we are told to repress it rather than deepen and redirect it. Many a man has tried to become "soft" at the expense of facing the true power present in himself. When that happens we turn outward in violence or inward in despair. Men have notoriously identified with what they do rather than experience themselves in the depths of their being. That takes a commitment to a journey inwards which is as demanding and hazardous as any adventure in the outer world. Men have been the ones to go to war, to prison, and settle matters with brute force.

- Power—do you believe you can make a difference? Where do you need to challenge the sense of powerlessness which is robs you of initiative and purpose?
- Identity—do you identify yourself rather narrowly with your small circle in your work—or are you willing to embrace a larger and, sometimes, disturbing vision?
- Contention—how do you handle differences and difficulties? How do we raise difficult issues and talk about them? What do we need to do to level with each other? What can we do to engage in uncompromising straight talk?
- Learning—how do you deal with new ideas? The temptation is to stay in the comfort zone and resist new challenges from the outside.

Richard Pascale goes on to point out that each of these four indicators move between death-dealing and life-bearing practices. Power moves between resignation ("I can't make a difference and nothing will ever change") to possibility ("I am open to the future because the future is God's"). Identity moves between isolation and separation to solidarity—being truly the Body of Christ. Contention moves between avoidance and deadlock to open conversation and commitment. Learning moves between being static and self-confirming and self-satisfied to openness to new ideas, possibilities and initiatives.

David points out with inescapable clarity the social reality of being human. We exist only in relationship. In religious terms we might say that God is making of us, all of us, a holy family—not a sort of holy card vision of the family but a picture of a family which is messier and more wonderful than we would like, more unruly and less elegant than a holy picture, and far more real. One of the annoyances of many books on spirituality is that they rarely bridge the gap between our aspirations and our actual lives.

The best image I've found for this Holy Family comes from the writings of Lionel Blue, an English rabbi who, like David James, writes elegantly and eloquently about the human condition. Rabbi Blue, just after the Second World War, was Convener of Beth Din, which is the Reform Jewish Ecclesiastical Court. Trying to apply the rules, some of them archaic, to actual situations, was very hard for him. He writes, "As we listened to our clients' stories, we realized what a gap had grown up between our pre-war religion and post-war reality." While rules are important, but people don't fit as neatly as we would like into the rules. Because the job of ecclesiastical lawyer was somewhat restricting and claustrophobic, Rabbi Blue decided, with a refugee friend Eva, to found an unusual congregation. It was a kind of mirror image of the Ecclesiastical Court. There were no forms to fill in, and everyone was welcome.

"No questions were asked about anyone's religious status, or about their personal relationships, whether single, divorced, or bereaved-or with no marriages at all. If they wanted a Jewish Sabbath evening with candles, cinnamon cakes, company and blessings, they were welcome, and if they did not they could walk out whenever they wished. We also asked them to add something to the supper table if they could. They were all kinds, even some well-set-up Jews, pillars-of-society Jews, Jews living with Protestants, Catholics, Buddhists, and Jews who kept very non-kosher company indeed-and of course their partners came too, and received an even bigger welcome, not to convert them but because they might feel strange. There were half-Jews, quarter-Jews, one-eighth Jews. To these we added a Christian evangelical choir, who were so decent that they didn't try to convert anyone there, except by being the decent Christians that they were." An odd assortment of people including one man "who said he was the Holy Spirit and locked himself in the broom cupboard, and some who took one look at us and left in disgust."

Here was the synagogue for the unqualified! One I would like to join. Rabbi Blue concludes, "I could have cried with relief: at last, I had found a temporary religious home, and Judaism was doing what is does best: turning the religious ragtag and bobtail of a big city into a family. Into even a sort of Holy Family." I think this is what many men need and want today. David James' book is rather like an encouraging letter from an older and wiser brother who, having made his own mistakes and messes, wants to support his brothers. Here is a handbook for the Synagogue of the Unqualified.

Alan Jones
Dean of Grace Cathedral
San Francisco

Preface

We are one of the most educationally driven nations in the world. Institutions which masquerade as "pre-pre-schools" handle children— beginning at six months of age—all day long across our country. From there, we graduate to kindergarten and begin the long trek through elementary, junior and senior high school. Then we go to junior college or university for more years than we care to count. If we don't opt for "higher education," we can still attend trade school; massage institutes, driver's education, beauty school, bartending courses, dog-training academies, martial-arts dojos, or real estate schools. We can invest our time and money in a variety of educational adventures from the sublime (conservatories of art and music) to the ridiculous ("Success and Influence Academies").

All of this points to the affluence and ease of much of our society: people have enough money to advance their pool of knowledge. Yet, it also reduces the role of education to job preparation. Once upon a time, a university student was destined to learn the classics, philosophy, art and music to prepare them for *life*. Today we grab a quick M.B.A. or a beautician's license and set off to make as much money as we possibly can before anyone else makes it ahead of us. Where once we took satisfaction, if not pleasure, from being under the tutelage of a master, now we sue our professors when he or she refuses to inflate our grade to keep up our grade point average.

This materialistic view of one's vocation sheds light not only upon the poverty of our educational philosophy, but also upon the tepid spiritual pulse that our country subsists upon. It's almost an article of faith that satisfaction in life comes from gathering as many things to ourselves as we can. So, to "go for it all" means that we have to figure out a way to get all "that we deserve." Everyone and everything else, including God, become a means to the end of my hunger for status, which I think that wealth will provide. Knowledge becomes a commodity to be used like everything else on our quest for success.

I'm not against education; I am a priest, therapist and graduate school professor, so my wall is cluttered with degrees and certificates. But I have realized, perhaps too late, that no amount of education will ever guarantee that I will become a wise man. No spiritual tradition of any depth or vibrancy ever reduced education to vocational training. On the contrary, the human experience across the millennia held that to learn something was to share, somehow, in the life of God. In the Hebrew Scriptures the admonishment was for God's people to seek Wisdom with their entire being, for it is Wisdom, the personification of God that ordered life and settled the soul. Christianity is replete with exhortations to share in God's wisdom through the gifts and fruit of the Holy Spirit.

Wisdom, as I am defining it, is the membrane that joins our knowledge and life experience to a context of universal meaning and purpose. When we seek wisdom, we come to know not only how to read the schematic of life, we also learn to feel it's texture and purpose because we draw deeply from the source of life that is God. Education can probably tell us the "how" of anything under the sun, but it pales to the stunning beauty of wisdom's "why." Education can fill the mind with unlimited bits of stainless steel data, but wisdom will illuminate the heart with purpose, direction and meaning.

Admittedly, these comparisons paint with a very broad brush. However, education alone never produces great people and our age needs eminent men and women like few before. The oft-tragic tale of human history points to the disastrous results of education cut off from wisdom. Experiments conducted by Nazi's on helpless Jews and the computer-directed killing of innocents in any modern war bares witness to the inability of knowledge alone to usher in an age of beneficence. Wisdom, that is, sharing in God's life and love in the particulars of the "here and now," holds the best chance to find any solution to the complex moral and ethical dilemmas which beset us.

Earlier cultures knew that wisdom didn't just fall from the heaven into the minds and heart of their young. It was the job of the elders to initiate children into the mysteries of life in a way that rooted them to both God and culture. Using sacred stories, scriptures and rituals, the community ensured that their young would know how to make sense out of both life's tragedies and successes. We have precious little of that today. Men and women, struggling to make ends meet, find themselves as strangers to each other at the end of a workday and they have little time for anything to do with children. Beside their classic function of education, schools have become day care facilities, health centers, and restaurants rolled into one conglomerate of service because parents have abdicated their role as primary provider for their children.

In my work with men and spirituality, I've discovered a deep yearning among men for an initiation into the realm of wisdom. On retreat's and in workshops I ask men to look back on their lives and list five things *that they know now*, that they wished their father's had taught them in childhood. After some time to reflect and share with others, men inevitably share a desire for the simple, yet profound lessons of life…they want to drink deeply from wisdom's well. A common theme for men is that while their father's may or may not have given them a home and some form of education, few taught their sons how to live.

After listening to hundreds of men for five years now, I decided to try and tackle the question of men, life and wisdom. In my first book, *"What Are They Saying About Masculine Spirituality?"* I took only a cursory glance at the role of elders and young people. So, to write this book, I decided to wrestle with my own life questions and those of my clients, parishioners and collogues in an attempt to offer a simple way into wisdom.

In these fifty-two reflections, the reader will find simple reflections upon lessons that men struggle with, from the purpose of lives to our relationship to women and work. My hope is that men will read this book and try to teach the lessons to their children. But even more importantly, I want men to make each reflection his own in a way that makes fits his own journey. The Book of Common Prayer has a prayer that asks God to help us "read, mark, learn and inwardly digest" the scriptures. If we can do the same to the wisdom that seeps out from behind my meager words, then we will leave a rich legacy of wisdom for our children to grow into. I believe that this legacy is not only our privilege as Christian men, it is our obligation and our children will suffer if we don't.

Each of my reflections is grounded in my experience as a follower of Jesus Christ, the Bible and the lived tradition of the Christian Church. I believe that Christianity is a wisdom tradition and that Jesus' teachings and life have implications for everyone who peruses this book. Having said this, though, I've tried to cast a wider vision than that of many partisan Christian writings today. Hopefully, I've written a book that a non-Christian person could read without cringing and benefit from as I've drawn from several religious traditions to complete this work. For as the book of Proverbs says, "Wisdom cries out on the street corner to anyone who will hear." (1:20). So let's walk together, open our ears, eyes and heart and see what treasures Wisdom has in store for us.

1

Life is Not Fair

"Were it possible for us to see further than our knowledge reaches, perhaps we would endure our sadness with greater confidence than our joys. For they are moments when something new has entered into us, something unknown."
Rainer Maria Rilke

We live in a culture where identifying myself as a victim has become something of an art form. Rather than take responsibility for the choices of our lives, looking for another to blame has become fashionable and is easier than growing up. If we're lucky, we're able to sue somebody for every penny they've got and land a guest appearance on a television talk show as well! When we can't find a suitable person or situation to indict for our disaster, we begin asking the larger questions of equity. Like Job, we cry out in anguish, "Why did this happen to me?" Variations on this theme are "I don't deserve this," and "it's not fair!" The underlying assumption is, of course, that life should be fair, at least for me, if not you. For many this translates into a vague but real belief that I should get whatever I want. Life must grant me every opportunity for success, open every door of privilege, free me from every vestige of suffering, and ensure that I have comfort and meaning for the rest of my life. When these don't happen, anguish pulsates through my soul and self-justified anger begins to boil beneath the surface.

There are at least two problems inherent with this perspective. First, *life isn't fair*. We weave the tapestry of our days with joy and sorrow, praise and blame, honor and shame, gain and loss. Jesus promised "tribulation in this world" and the writers of the Hebrew Scriptures recall how sorrow and difficulty are the inheritance of all. In native cultures a primary purpose of initiation rituals was to teach young boys to expect difficulty in life. We recoil may in horror at the brutality of this ritual wounding, but for the rest of their lives, the young men carried a reminder that life was going to be tough. By contrast, modern culture deludes our children into believing that nothing should stand in their way as a matter of principle. So we have an emerging class of young people who have a simmering resentment etched upon their heart.

Next, by demanding fairness from life we rob ourselves of the growth that comes from encountering difficulties of soul. In his reflections upon the path to wholeness, M. Scott Peck puts it this way:

> "Problems are the cutting edge that distinguishes between success and failure. Problems call forth our courage and our wisdom; indeed, they create our courage and our wisdom. It is only because of problems that we grow mentally and spiritually."[1]

When we view the tribulations of life as opportunities to strengthen and liberate our heart, new possibilities of love, service and relationship arise. The collision of our needs, hopes and dreams with the reality of our life opens new vistas of understanding and purpose. So, the choice becomes clear, we can run from them and blame everyone else for our trouble. Or we can see them for the invitation into maturity that they are. Then with St. Paul we can say:

We boast in our afflictions, knowing that they bring about perseverance;
and perseverance, proven character;
and proven character, hope;
and hope does not disappoint
Romans 5: 3-5

> **If we grow in direct proportion to our ability to encounter and work with the inevitable difficulties of our lives, shouldn't we teach our children how to do the same?**

2

Service Brings Significance

"You will find, as you look back upon your life, that the moments which stand out are the moments when you have dome things for others." Henry Drummond

Drive along any highway in America and pay attention to the bumper stickers plastered on the cars that pass by. Eventually you'll find one that proudly proclaims, "He who dies with the most toys wins." This axiom exposes one of our most cherished (and deadly) cultural illusions: that the quantity of our collections measures the value of our life. Our almost instinctual response is to reply, "well of course they don't!" Yet is that true? Isn't there a part of us that look at the various "things" that we have accumulated with a self-validating pride? A good way to tell is to go through your closets and see what you could absolutely live without. You'll be amazed at the amount of things that we don't need. The more-is-better syndrome has captured the imagination of so many of us that it has almost become an article of faith in our capitalistic society. Even within the Church there has been an explosion of the "prosperity gospel." Watch television long enough and you're likely to run across evangelists who teach that poverty is a sign of our faithlessness and God's displeasure. So now, the followers of Jesus, who had nowhere to

14

lay his head, claim material abundance as their rights while 40,000 starve to death each day.

The pursuit of "more" as the way to find happiness and satisfaction is both an illusion and dead-end. Its illusory power lies in the promise that if I can just get that next car, boat, painting, spouse or home, I'll find inner satisfaction. The problem, of course, is that an outer world solution will never work in the inner world. This is why the pursuit of things for their own sake is a dead end. When all is said and done, *nothing* can satisfy us. The abundance of wealthy people in psychotherapy, who struggle with addictions or are simply miserable, gives testimony to the inability of *things* to provide inner peace. Yet, as a culture we pursue adornments, toys and status symbols with an unrelenting passion because there is a gnawing emptiness within which we hope the next purchase will assuage.

Those people most at peace with themselves have discovered that while it's pleasant to be comfortable, what satisfies are relationships that are meaningful and the difference that they make in the lives of others. Whether they work in Calcutta's slums, cancer wards at the local hospital, migrant literacy classes, or quietly within the network of their own home, people who freely give of themselves are happy. In other words, the ability to make a significant contribution to our family, school, workplace, church, or community projects brings much more gratification than collecting trophies to our adolescent ego.

Remember the story of the minister who was standing by the graveside of the famously wealthy man after conducting the funeral service. An admirer of the tycoon asked the pastor, "How much did he leave?" Without batting an eye, the minister replied, "Why all of it, of course!"

Do not store up for yourselves treasures on earth, where moth and decay destroy,
and where thieves break in and steal.
Instead, store up for yourselves treasures in heaven,
where neither moth nor decay destroys, nor thieves do not break in and steal;
for where your treasure is, there will be your heart also.
Matthew 6:20-21

Look at your motivations today. Are you working to provide for your family and to contribute to the common good, or are you "out for yourself?" Your children will follow your lead.

3

Your Deeds Reveal the Real You

"Men should be what they seem." Shakespeare

While browsing through the advertisement section of a business maga-zine, I was amazed at the number of courses that one can take to become a more effective communicator. Personal Growth Consultants offer a plethora of workshops, seminars, books and tapes to help you polish your communication skills. What accounts for this explosion in communication technologies? Research polls consistently show that public speaking is one of the deepest fears of people today. It seems we'd rather undergo painful and debilitating surgery than stand up in front of a group of people and risk their judgment and rejection. Developing the ability to speak with precision and effectiveness is a skill that serves us well in the world of family, business or church.

A man I deeply admire spends his free time working with inner-city young people teaching them how to be effective public speakers. He points out with great pride how these young people glimmer with a new hope and possibility just by learning to speak well in public. Their sense of self-worth increases when they ascend a personal mountain that few in their neighborhood will. From this vantage point, they find it easier to believe in themselves and their ability to enter the world with confidence.

Yet, as with everything that is good, we must be aware of the shadow side of the human development movement. Author and organizational consultant Stephen Covey points to the danger of cosmetic improvement within our culture. He notes that without a change in the essential personality, teaching someone how to communicate effectively is counterproductive, because then all you have is a smooth-talking scoundrel on your hands.

All of this points to the theme for today's lesson. The way we live our life, our interactions with others, how we spend our time and resources are a more telling evidence of who we are than the words we use. If we lace our heart with dishonesty, self-seeking and malice, these will eventually brim to the surface in our relationships with others. Emerson knew this when he said, "Who you are shouts so loud that I can't hear what it is that you're saying." In other words, no matter how precise our language, skillful our presentation, or fine-tuned our public persona; our actions will eventually give us away. We can probably keep the facade up for quite a while, but as with an unsafe building, all it will take is one jolt to bring your life crashing down. Certainly others will spot the difference between our words and our deeds long before we do, and much to our chagrin, our children often see us more clearly than we see ourselves. So it is imperative that we offer them visions of authentic manhood.

Conversion of the heart becomes, therefore, the act of supreme importance. By God's grace, we can undertake the necessary journey of self-discipline, prayer and authentic living that heals the heart and bridges the chasm between deed and word.

By their fruits you will know them.
Do people pick grapes from thorn bushes, or figs from thistles?
Just so, every good tree bears good fruit; and a rotten tree bears bad fruit.
A good tree cannot bear bad fruit any more than a bad tree bear good fruit.
Matthew 7: 16-18

What actions will betray your words today?
Are they part of the memories you want to pass on to your children?

4

Women Don't Exist for Your Entertainment.

"The truth will set you free, but first it will make you miserable." James Garfield

Believe it or not, women have a right to exist apart from you! This is a revelation for many men. Popular culture teaches that from childhood, a woman's purpose in life is to nourish, comfort and entertain men. In some ways, it's easy to see how we fall into this trap. Our mother was the source of our nourishment, comfort and esteem. If we were beautiful in Mom's eyes, then we have a sparkle today. If rejected or disdained by her, we struggle with that rejection in a deep way and we carry that wound for the better part of our lives. Men carry about an image of the feminine world within them sparked largely by their relationship with Mother. This *anima* awakens our hearts and inspires us toward all that is beautiful. Yet, for all the beauty of the feminine world, we harbor great misgivings in our relationships with it.

Men have an ambivalence toward women that is well known. We love the women in our lives, but often don't want to get too close to them. We yearn for feminine sensual comforts, but we want it on our terms, not theirs. If left in the darkness of our unconscious, this can lead to the abuse of that which we cherish. Whether physical or verbal, when we use women for our comfort, sensuality or security, we say, "You are not a person with your own life, love, dreams and possibilities. You exist for me."

What is not as well known is that this ambivalence toward women is most often rooted in our fear of them. From time immemorial, we have perceived women as a powerful threat to our vitality and life energy. In his book "Lying with the Heavenly Woman," Psychologist Robert Johnson offers concise and telling insights into man's battle to overcome controlling influences of the feminine in his life. He remarks:

> "The knights of old donned their helmets and armor, swords and lances, and went out to conquer the world, 'out there.' The modern hero faces a wealth of possibilities in a new form—the bewildering array of interior feminine elements, which he must rescue, nurture, woo and protect."[2]

We desperately want women to nurture and satisfy us. The paradox is, of course, is that while we're afraid they won't, we're also terrified that they might, because in either case, we fear their control over us. Sometimes we seduce women, sometimes we fight them and sometimes we abandon them because we are afraid that they are going to overwhelm us and in so doing, reveal the very weakness that run from.

This attitude keeps everyone enslaved. When we deny women the right and dignity of full personhood by turning them into consumable objects, we diminish the flow of divine love for all. It's easy to forget that women are co-heirs of God's image. As a matter of fact, that's why they are so attractive to us: we see in them a glimpse of God's beauty that we haven't recognized anywhere else. When we idolize them, we denigrate both our sisters and the God who created them. Our fear traps us in co-dependent webs of relationships that stymie our own growth as men of purpose and distinction. In other words, we all lose.

There is no fear in love, for perfect love drives out fear.
1st John 4:18

Are women worthy of your respect, love and dignity or are they only valuable when they make you feel good?

5

Discipline Leads to Joy

"What we do upon some great occasion will probably depend on what we already are: and what we are will be the result of previous years of self-discipline."
H.P. Liddon

One of the things that men admire about professional athletes is their capacity for discipline, self-sacrifice and commitment to their sport. We know that while raw talent is essential, the countless hours on the practice field, in the weight room and studying the strategy of opposing teams which brings the victory. A man's capacity for personal discipline is not restricted to our athletic endeavors alone. From the corporate world to social activism, men exhibit a dedication, determination and drive which builds nations, creates art and has unleashed a torrent of creativity throughout history.

Mythologists call this capacity for drive and discipline "Warrior Energy." It is an internal energy which enables us to undertake great challenges in the face of terrible opposition, to persevere when exhausted and remain committed to a personal code of conduct despite the outcome. Warrior energy, like all instinctual drives can go awry and that's where the necessity for personal discipline comes in. Our psychic impulses, if left unchecked, can overflow into addictions, compulsions and destructive behavior. So consistent self-discipline serves as a channel for these deeply personal and powerful drives.

Discipline also frees us from the enslaving grasp of our habits. We know that the ways we respond to situations are in large part habitual. If someone cuts in front of me on the freeway and I lapse into road rage, the odds are that errant drivers have irritated me for a long time. If I have a drink every night at 5:00, it's probably as much custom as need. Our habits are the enemy of a soulful and authentic life, for they rob us of the capacity for spontaneity, passion and joy. One author calls the practice of self-discipline, or the ability to delay gratification, the "Sacred No" because personal discipline is a gift given that we might experience peace of mind, personal satisfaction and joy.

In his helpful work entitled, *"The Celebration of Discipline,"* Richard Foster points to the ultimate goal of the disciplined life:

> "Joy is the keynote of all the Disciplines. The purpose of the Disciplines is liberation from the stifling slavery to self-interest and fear. When the inner spirit is liberated from all that weighs it down, it can hardly be described as dull and drudgery. Singing, dancing, even shouting characterize the Disciplines of the spiritual life."[3]

Our sons and daughters need disciplined men in their lives. If we fail to teach others how to receive the grace and gift of personal discipline, we will watch as their physical, moral and spiritual life will atrophy into irrelevance. Without the boundaries and channels for their personal energy, they will be lost in the confusing swirl of addiction, sorrow and despair. The next generation cannot afford men held captive to every whim and passion that comes their way.

For God did not give us a spirit of cowardice, but rather
a spirit of power and of love and of self-discipline.
2nd Timothy 1:7

Who is the master of my soul?
Spirit-graced discipline, or childish habit?

6

Simplicity Liberates!

"Life is not complex, we are complex.
Life is simple and the simple thing is the right thing." Oscar Wilde

It seems that harmony, peace of mind and stability have been lost in the frantic pace of our technological era. We live in a time of complexity where conflict, confusion and rancor are a significant part of the social fabric. Feeling overwhelmed at the momentum of society is common for many people. It's easy to understand this psychic discomfort. The information coming at us every day is beyond our capacity to process it. The frenetic quality to life manifests in our music, media, sports and recreation. For the first time in our culture, the word "Extreme" is used positively in advertising to portray an optimum state of stimulation or quantity. Violence has become a spectator sport and our children are becoming increasingly callous to its effects on television and in our neighborhoods.

We respond to the complexity of life in different ways. Many escape into mindless entertainment, trying to "shut down," while others embrace the excessive activities of our culture, looking for the next thrill. No choice along this continuum brings maturity, stability or peace to the soul. So, we ask the question, "Is there a way to restore the harmony which we've lost?"

A consistent theme of the spiritual life is that embracing simplicity liberates us. A conscious choice to rid ourselves of the needless shackles of complexity is a courageous act of the heart demanding discipline, vision and prayer. It is helpful to see simplicity as a gift, a statement and a necessity. First, it is a gift freely given to all. After all, life is essentially simple. We were created to love God with every fiber of our being and to love everyone else with that same passion. Food is to be enjoyed, life to be celebrated and our heart opened to the thousand different ways that the Spirit leads us. The writer of Ecclesiastes reminds us that "God made man simple: man's complex problems are of his own devising." (7: 30 NAB) In other words, our complexity springs from ego-needs to feel important and special. We can never be "special enough" to slack the ego's craving, so we pile complexity upon dilemma and wonder why our spirit resists the burden.

This leads to the second characteristic of simplicity: it speaks volumes about the character of our relationship with God. When there is an abundance of soulful spirituality, our relationship with the outer world becomes less complex. Such spirituality has a ring of gospel freedom to it. It's impossible to find a person centered in God and overwhelmed with the fabric of life. They have developed a different perspective on what is important. A lifestyle of simplicity is a living parable of our movement toward a unified personality that leads to a plentitude of psychic energy and graciousness.

Finally, a lifestyle of simplicity is essential for our relationship with the rest of the world. Our ability to love God and others is limited by the amount of psychological and spiritual energy that we have to offer.

Simplicity, *the voluntary relinquishment of the extraneous,* liberates us to love and serve. We will never find peace of mind and heart without it.

If even the smallest things are beyond your control,
why do you worry about the rest?
Luke 12:26

Look at your life today.
What is essential? What nourishes and liberates you?
Do you really need the rest?

7

We See People Not As They Are, But As We Are

"Humankind cannot bear too much reality." T.S. Elliot

Conversion is a central theme in the spiritual life. The need to stop long enough to look at life, see where our actions are inconsistent with our vision and make necessary change is a universal religious principle. Christian history is replete with examples of men and women who have experienced those movements of graced conversion for which we all so deeply yearn. The testimony of people who have struggled with life's burdens and discovered liberation, peace of mind and a purpose for their lives abound within the Church, and without it. For example, 12-Step recovery programs lead people to sobriety through a conscious evaluation of their life, the honest support of others and a daily commitment to sobriety.

We can never come to wholeness or authenticity until we understand how we shade life with the subtleties and complexities of our personal history. If I am a middle-class white male, a sub-Saharan peasant woman, the Pope, a trash collector in Manhattan, a terrorist, a concert violinist or an indigenous shaman, my experience frames the way I relate to God, others and myself. As such, my family traditions, cultural bias, religious perspective, political orientation and psychological makeup all contribute to my relationship with the world.

A gospel conversion calls us to begin the arduous process of learning to see beyond our own agendas and prejudices to embrace the love and justice of God. Without a fundamental understanding of the fact that I see, in large part, what I have been conditioned to see, such conversion is impossible. St. Paul's life offers a stunning picture of this type of conversion. As an emissary of the Pharisees, he journeys to Damascus to persecute a group of people so vile and dangerous that they threaten the social order. Armed with what is essentially a license to kill, this religious fundamentalist is intent upon destroying this menacing sect. Suddenly, in a blinding encounter with the God of love, his entire word view is shaken and, in time, he sees the fledgling Christian community not as enemies, but as his beloved. This is a crucial understanding for our development as men of the Spirit. We judge people as good or bad, worthy or despised, not by their action or inaction as much as upon priorities and prejudices formed in large part, by the world in which we live

Our culture is in the midst of a battle for its identity. The word "Balkinization," connoting the segregation and scapegoating of people different from us, has entered our common vocabulary, sometimes with a literal vengeance. Without an experience of liberating Gospel vision we remain trapped within the confinement of our very human, and limited, limited worldview.

If you were blind, you would have no sin;
but since you are saying, 'We see,' your sin remains.
John 9: 41

> **Who carries your projections today?**
> **Will you ask God to see them as they actually are?**

8

Discover Your Pantheon of Heroes

"Without heroes we are all plain people and don't know how far we can go."
Bernard Malmud

Stories have always fascinated people. Long before the explosion of technology and media, we expressed the truth of the human experience through myths, fairy tales, legends, folklore and drama. Even today, images and feelings that emerge from stories touch us in ways that the dry, linear, written word cannot. Movie theaters around the world take in hundreds of millions of dollars every weekend. While part of this may spring from our need to escape from life for 90 minutes, it is also likely that our soul still yearns to be spoken to through a story. We've taken storytelling to its pinnacle of technical excellence, but ultimately, a good movie reveals the human mystery in a way that fascinates, inspires and challenges us. This is why Frederico Fellini says that "The Cinema like all other manifestations of creativity, out to be in a state of combustion, a metabolism of the unconscious, a journey toward the center of ourselves and the world."

Spiritual masters have always known this. Finding a teacher that doesn't use stories to convey deep truth is impossible. Jesus use of parables was a common teaching practice for a rabbi of his time. Yet he isn't alone. Spiritual literature employs the language of image and symbol to express something at the deeply transcendent level. It's almost as though the psyche refuses to accept archetypal truth unless it comes in the dynamic figure of stories. They allow us to identify with its characters, and yet, give us a safe space so we don't get overwhelmed by their power. Joseph Campbell spoke to the power of mythology when he said that stories help us find the clues of life within ourselves.

One of the most powerful stories available to form the young person's consciousness is the biography. Telling stories of courageous men and women not only inspires us, it opens a level of deep resonance within which can imprint their memory upon us forever. This is why the lives of the saints were such an inspiring force for young Catholics and why many Protestant kids love the dramatic tales of the Hebrew Scriptures. The accounts of men and women who triumphed over adversity are as responsible for the conversion of millions as any well-delivered sermon has ever been.

In primitive cultures, passing on the great traditions from elder to younger occurred in sacred settings, usually through the motif of the great stories of the tribe. The elders linked the young people to the tribe through recounting the archaic stories of the ancestors. The closest we come to this today is found in the halls of our national military academies where we have enshrined the names, images and stories of war heroes to inspire loyalty and devotion.

We would do well to examine our hearts to see who is in our own "Hall of Fame." If they are truly heroes, their recollection will invoke awe and respect while inspiring us to follow their path to glory. If they don't, they may serve as an object lesson for some other time, but they're not heroes'. Men and women worth memorializing will inspire us to nobility and service. The stories of those who have gone before us, point the way to a life filled with meaning, challenge, contribution and satisfaction. Help your children discover the great ones as well, for they lead to conversion of heart and holiness of deed.

I have not time to tell of those who by faith conquered kingdoms, did what was righteous, obtained the promises, closed the mouths of lions, put out raging fires, escaped the devouring sword; became strong in battle and turned back foreign invaders. Hebrews 11: 32b-34

> **What great stories enchanted you as a boy?**
> **How can you introduce your family to them?**

9

Develop a Prayer Life that Changes You, Not Them

*"Prayer may not change things for you,
but it sure changes you for things."* Samuel Shoemaker

If you've been living in a spiritual and social vacuum for the past few years, you might not have noticed that prayer has become an acceptable topic of conversation again. The fascinating thing is that praying isn't limited to religious circles anymore. For example, Larry Dossey has reintroduced the medical world to the efficacy of prayer as a healing technique and meditation has gone "mainstream." There was a time where, if you spoke publicly about prayer, mainstream culture looked at you a bit warily. Certainly there was always some form of obligatory prayer at the beginning of legislative sessions. Yet it seemed that this "prayer" was akin to playing the National Anthem at the beginning of a ball game, a nostalgic nod to a more honorable past. No one took it seriously enough to believe God might be listening!

Unfortunately, Christian people are often the source of public ambivalence about prayer. Our practical understanding of prayer contributes to this apprehension since we often ask God to endorse our sectarian and political agendas with little concern for the common good. Prayer devolves into "me and mine" appealing to God to answer our prayers at the expense of others. An adolescent example of this principle is when both teams at a football team praying for victory: whom does God love more? Asking God to smite our enemies is more an indictment of our own judgments than a prayer that Jesus would utter. We also reduce God in prayer to a "divine bellhop" who is obligated to give me what I want, when I want, if I use the correct formula. All of this seems very self-serving and untrustworthy to those who watch from afar and it distorts the true meaning of the prayer of petition and intercession.

These notions are actually alien to a gospel understanding of prayer. A more helpful way of looking at prayer might be that we take the time *to make ourselves present to God who is already lovingly present to us.* In this encounter of presence, sometimes fueled by petition, sometimes by praise, and sometimes by silence, we are transformed. Each of us has a place in our heart where we have uttered an emphatic "no" to God's loving invitation. In the days before his death, Cardinal Joseph Bernadin marveled at the "no" within his own heart:

> "I have desperately wanted to open the door of my soul as Zacchaeus opened the door of his house. Only in that way can the Lord take over my life completely. Yet many times in the past I have only let him come in part of the way. I talked with him, but seemed afraid to let him take over. Why was I afraid? Why did I open the door only so far and no more?"[4]

An authentic experience of prayer heals our heart and gives us the courage to turn the "no" of our ego into a surrendered "yes" to God. Jesus teaches that authentic moments of transformation occur when we finally discover our need for God's presence in our lives. The prayer of transformation recognizes that we don't have as many answers as we think and we invite God to heal, teach and lead us. Then, from a place of spiritual realignment and conversion, we enter God's yearning for the healing and salvation of the world.

The world needs men of deep prayer, those profoundly connected with the heart of God. Embark on a journey the place of transformative prayer where God will touch, heal and change *you*.

The prayer of the lowly pierces the clouds;
it does not rest till it reaches its goal.
Sirach 35:17

Do you pray with your family?
Does they see you making demands of God or entering into a deeper relationship with the Spirit?

10

Freedom is a Choice, Not a circumstance

"The secret of happiness is freedom,
and the secret of freedom is courage." Thulydides

Anthony de Mello told the story of a lion who was captured and put in a concentration camp with other lions. The new prisoner toured the camp and was amazed to find that the lions had developed social groups. The lions were fully adjusted to captivity and had established a virtual society within the camp. Looking about, he saw lions that were politicians, artists, musicians, healers, philosophers and laborers. Yet, the most intriguing lion was one that sat apart from the others on a rock, gazing out at the fence in the distance. When he asked the other lions about the solitary figure on the rock, they warned him to keep away as he was a troublemaker. One day his curiosity finally got the better of him and he approached the fence watcher and asked what he was doing. The lion offered nothing by way of reply to the question. Finally, in exasperation, the newly captive lion demanded to know what he was doing and why he spent all his time looking at the fence. "Shhh," replied the contemplative one, "I'm looking for a way out."

A profound cultural illusion ingrained in most everyone's belief systems is that our circumstances are responsible for our state of mind. As with other lessons in this book, the very statement of the problem stirs up feelings of disbelief and for some, revulsion. Yet, if we examine the way we relate to the world around us, many would have to admit that there is more than a little truth to the statement. Few want to admit that anyone but themselves is in control of their emotional life. After all, self-determination is supposed to be the epitome of the American lifestyle.

Sadly, this is not so. Many of us have become as captive to forces outside ourselves as the lions in the story. We have given people the power to control our emotional lives because we think that they can make us happy or sad, angry or joyful by their actions toward us. The advertising industry understands this principle of human behavior. Their not so subtle strategy is to convince you that without this deodorant or these shoes, you will be ugly, intellectually inferior, banished from society and less than acceptable. Tony Robbins calls this "Neuro-Associative Conditioning," the practice of using emotional associations to reinforce desired thought patterns. In other words, if advertisers can get you to link enough pleasure to buying a certain product and enough pain too not having it, then it's sold before you can race to the store.

People who triumph over the circumstances of life inspire us. Holocaust survivors, those who overcome disease or find new life in the midst of pain give testimony to the truth that *circumstances don't create us, they define us*. Everyone who finds the ability to transcend a personal difficulty is one who understands that the genius to life is found within, not without. Henry David Thoreau put it best when he remembered that "Things do not change, we do." So both the good and bad news today is that you are the master of your own emotional destiny.

You will know the truth and it will set you free
John 8:32

Have you given people permission to hold you hostage to their
emotional needs?
Who is responsible for your emotions, if not you?

11

Today is All You Have

"Life is nothing but a series of moments. Start living the moments and the years will take care of themselves." Gary Fenchuk

Goals have become gods to many in our success-oriented culture. The ability to set priorities and direct our efforts is often the sign of good stewardship, for without them nothing of value gets accomplished. Even in the spiritual life, personal disciplines like prayer, meditation, fasting, scripture reading, journal keeping and worship need the protective structures of focused attention to keep them in place. For example, we will never realize the desire to have a meaningful prayer life without making it a disciplined objective. Our ability to put our best efforts off for relative goods of comfort and ease is no surprise to anyone who has begun a new endeavor. The principle of homeostasis tells us that an organism will always try to return to its original state rather than change. This is why almost every personal development workshop teaches goal setting. Without the guiding light of our goals, we can't see through the darkness of inertia and procrastination.

While appreciating the focus that goal setting provides, it's also safe to say that it has relative value for the spiritual life. Goals can keep us so oriented toward some future of final accomplishment that we forget to live today. A life grounded in soulful spirituality is lived in the "now" of every moment. The thoughts, dreams, fantasies, challenges, hatreds, fears and desires that we experience all take place in "this moment." As such, the present is where healing and redemption, or sin and loss occur. Much of our distress comes from living through either past memory or future anticipation. It's as though we become captive to thoughts that have no relationship to any experience in the present. A person battling with recovery once said, "If I'm depressed, it's because I'm living in the past, and if I'm anxious, it's because I'm living in the future."

The human experience is fraught with a variety of emotions and feelings, some of which are quite painful. While we enjoy life's pleasurable sensations, we recoil from the painful ones. Who wouldn't? No matter how you slice it, a painful experience is agonizing. So we avoid the present with both its pain and joy. Living in either the past or future is one way of hiding from the invitation of the moment. This limits God's grace and our ability to find meaning for our experience. Alan Jones writes:

> "When pain and wonder are experienced together, a secret begins to emerge with regard to the possible significance of our lives. The secret is very simple: living means giving. True living requires surrender. If we really want to live, we have to find some means of giving ourselves away. We have a choice in the face of wonder and pain. We can repress the secret of surrender and live a life that is marked and marred by a rhythm of self-justification, or we can go on the pilgrimage

of sacrifice and surrender. We can wall up the heart, or we can give it away."[5]

Because of this, the only goal that makes sense from a spiritual point of view is to love both God and others with an unquenchable passion in every moment of your life. Are you looking for a vibrant meaningful life? You will find it only today. Yesterday is gone and tomorrow doesn't exist. Open yourself to experience today with all of its joy and sorrow, gain and loss, praise and blame. Anything else is illusion.

This is the day that the Lord has made, Let us rejoice and be glad in it!
Psalm 118:24

Take some time today to discover the ways you escape from present moments.
Do you flee into the past, charge toward the future or fantasize in this present?

12

Learn to Lament

"Prayer is not asking. It is a longing of the soul." Mahatma Gandhi

Real men do cry, but you might not think so if you listen to the banter in locker rooms, bars or Rotary Clubs. We have moments when the eye glistens and the heart softens, but we quickly catch ourselves and wipe away our awkward display of emotion before anyone spots us in a moment of weakness. Actually, this stereotype is not quite true. Spend time at the Vietnam War Memorial and you'll see warriors sobbing with uncontrollable grief. Attend the daily funerals of children murdered in our inner cities and you will discover men writhing in agony. While we are capable of grief, there is a cultural bias against men opening their hearts this way. When he began to work with Men's retreats, Richard Rohr noticed that a primary task of masculine spirituality seems to be helping men to grieve. As a culture, we have little room for men's pain because it threatens our perceptions of strength and determination as the only "manly way."

If it's true that men haven't learned to grieve, it's also true that no one ever taught us how to lament, that is to cry out for others. As a result, our personal and communal spiritual life is tepid and lacks authenticity. Lamentation is a deep movement of the heart into the pain of the world. It is not necessarily concerned with our personal sorrows. My personal agony at the loss of a cherished one is painful, intense and unique, but is not necessarily lamentation. In my lamentation, I embrace the pain of our common life and make it my own. The prayer of lamentation recognizes the common injustices; pains and despairs from which it seems that only God can deliver us. The Hebrew Scriptures contrast these differences in the heartache of Job and the afflictions of Israel. The poetry of Job reflects a suffering that is personal, intense and debilitating, while the lamentations of Israel's prophets record the suffering of an entire people.

Three movements characterize the symphony of lamentation. First, when we lament, we share in God's pain for the world. In these moments, divine agony at the pain and injustice of people is poured out through us: we weep with God's tears. To lament is also to be prophetic. Our cry for justice points to the ways that we destroy each other in the pursuit of selfish and ego-driven agendas. Finally, it is a prayer of solidarity as we stand in the midst of the suffering ones. We cannot lament at a comfortable distance, we must embrace the experience of those who suffer and feel it as our own.

Even a cursory look reveals much in our society to lament today. Children starve to death in America and are murdered by their parents in record numbers. The working poor are unable to make enough money to provide necessities for their families. Despair, hopelessness and prejudice haunt the urban centers of our nation. Drugs, hatred and misunderstanding tear apart our families. Poor people and immigrants are the targets of middle-class anxiety and it has become secretly fashionable to scapegoat those different from us.

We are afraid of lamentation because it requires that we open our hearts to enter deeply into the world's suffering. Also, lamentation threatens us because it may reveal our own complacency for what it is: a willingness to let others suffer while we live in abundance. Until we learn to lament, our spirituality runs the risk of irrelevance because without it, we remain trapped in a world no bigger than ourselves.

Begin to lament, to mourn, to weep. Let your laughter be turned into mourning and your joy into dejection. James 4: 9

> **Have you ever deeply mourned for another's sorrow?**

13

There is Freedom in Forgiveness

"Forgiveness is man's deepest need and highest achievement." Horace Bushnell

Contrary to much of what passes for Christianity today, Jesus was primarily concerned about reconciliation, that is, the restoration of that which was lost or fractured. The scriptures record Jesus' passion for reconciliation in his teachings and actions. In the Sermon on the Mount, we see Jesus offering us a snapshot of God's desire for the world. According to Jesus, the poor, those who mourn, the meek, the righteous, the gentle, the merciful, the pure hearted, the peacemakers and the persecuted enjoy God's special favor. These categories have a dissonant ring in our success-conscious ears; yet, here we have God telling us that these folks have something to teach us. Perhaps it is because they have a head start on the rest of us in learning how to forgive. The poor don't often have recourse to attorneys or courts, so they have to learn how to let go and move on. In other words, they have to learn how to forgive.

Forgiveness is a foundational truth in the Christian Life. No matter what our religious practice, if we are serious about a life of faith, we first

46

must learn to forgive. We all know people who hold onto bitterness. Instead of moving through the process of forgiveness, they remain paralyzed in the bile of their own anger. The Christian, however, comes to peace of mind freedom of heart only through the corridor of forgiveness. In other words, if my heart cannot offer forgiveness, neither can I authentically receive it.

Part of the problem relates to our misunderstanding of forgiveness. We most often view forgiveness as either a legal act between people, or an occasion of mental amnesia. Properly understood, forgiveness actually is a process where we learn to let go of resentment, bitterness and ideas of revenge or hatred so *that we might be free!*

Two prevailing cultural illusions inhibit forgiveness today. First, many believe that forgiveness is for weaklings: that if you forgive someone then you're a "sucker." Most men are terrified of weakness, so this keeps forgiveness at a distance. Next, we've been taught that to forgive is to forget. Yet, often the wounds that we've received are so profound it seems that we won't ever forget them. Therefore we feel that if we can't forget, neither can we forgive.

Neither attitude is true. Forgiveness is a process of grieving where we release ourselves from the pain that controls us. As such, *forgiveness never depends on the other*: it is a decision on my part to be free. It doesn't matter whether the one who offended us gets the punishment they deserve, or even if they apologize. By forgiving them, I choose to release them and in doing so, I release myself. Otherwise I remain under the control of someone who hurt me in the past and continues to control me in the present.

A rabbi who was a holocaust survivor once met a man who had shared his prison cell in the concentration camp. Overjoyed to see his old companion, they talked for hours about their experiences of captivity.

Finally, the rabbi asked his friend how long it had taken him to forgive his captors. The man replied, "Forgive them? Never!" Shaking his head, the rabbi sadly noted, "If you've never forgiven them, I'm sorry, but they have you captive still."

If you forgive others their transgressions against you, your heavenly Father
will forgive you.
But if you do not forgive others, neither will your heavenly Father forgive
your transgressions.
Matthew 6:12

Who hurt you so deeply in the past that they still have you bound today?
Have you taught your children how to forgive someone who's hurt them?

14

Loving Your Enemies Is Not Only Possible, It's Necessary

"All, everything that I understand, I understand only because I love." Leo Tolstoy

Of all the precepts found in religious literature, the call to love our enemies is the most troubling, since it seems to go against the grain of human nature. After all, isn't it "natural" to hate those who hate us? The long and bloodied history of humanity answers with a resounding "yes!" It's hard to find an example of global conflict where reconciliation, not might, makes right. From the playground to the battlefield, our willingness to destroy those who disagree with us is a testament to the wounded condition of the human heart. This is not to say that we shouldn't resist evil when confronted by it. Other lessons in this book reflect upon creative alternatives to violence that the spiritual life offers.

The heart of the problem is not actually the use of force against our enemies. It's labeling people as enemies to begin with which places the soul in jeopardy. By declaring others my enemies, I launch a whole sequence of events that devalues and possibly destroys them. When I am convinced that you are the enemy, I summon the moral indignation necessary to justify any violence that I choose to inflict upon you.

Hitler's systematic annihilation of Jewish people is a stunning profile of the power of classifying others as the enemy. By convincing Germany that Jews were responsible for the problems in society, culture and religion, Hitler incited a surge of evil that slaughtered millions. As terrible as the Holocaust was, the process of demonizing and scapegoating continues with determination around the world today. Ethnic groups slaughter each other in the name of tribal allegiance, gang members destroy those who intrude upon their "territory" and a deadly breed of religious fundamentalism offers rewards for the execution of opponents.

The spirit of violence isn't limited to the killing fields, though: it permeates every human heart and institution. Politics in America thrives on the demonization of those who disagree with us to such an extent that honest discourse becomes difficult. Elections are won and lost, not on issues, but by inflaming voter's passions against "evil" opponents. Even in the Church, we take pleasure in finding faults with those who disagree with us, calling them heretic, reactionary, fascist, or unorthodox, and denying their fundamental dignity as a Child of God.

Jesus confronted this human darkness directly when he commanded, "Love your enemies." Knowing our propensity for spiritual dimwittedness, Jesus gave practical examples of this love. Not only are we to love as a lofty principle, but also we are to actively seek the good of those who go out of our way to hurt us. Why is this? First, loving our enemies is impossible apart from a movement of grace. This becomes therefore yet another opportunity for us to surrender to God's converting love, wisdom and justice. Secondly, given our predisposition to make enemies, perhaps the Lord knew that we need to come to grips with the judgment and fear that churns in the depth of our hearts. It's been said that we fear what we don't understand; we hate that which we fear and we destroy that which we hate. Jesus says this is not to be our way, do you believe him?

"You've heard it said, 'Love your neighbor and hate your enemy,'
But I say to you, Love your enemies and pray for those who persecute you,
that you may be children of your heavenly Father."
Matthew 5:43-45

Who have you labeled as an enemy in the depth of your own heart? If you view people of different races, creeds, religions or lifestyle as your "enemy" you poison your children's hearts as well.

15

Learn From Everyone

"In the spiritual life there are no enemies or friends…only teachers." David James

As any gourmet cook will tell you, a good meal depends, at least in part, on a good recipe. And for any recipe to work, you must have the right ingredients. The spiritual life is much like this: to have a life filled with purpose and authenticity, both our inner and outer lives must have a sense of balance and grace. A necessary component in a healthy spiritual life is a virtue that we might call "docility." Docility, the willingness to be taught, has fallen on hard times in popular culture. Our corporate ego is overwhelmed with self-importance and we're afraid that any attitude of humility betrays weakness. For all of their personality differences, people who exhibit a vibrancy and depth of spirit exhibit a common characteristic: they have an unquenchable desire to learn from everyone and everything.

The Christian life has been compared to a lifelong pilgrimage of learning. Many of us have gone to a spiritual conference or two and have come to the conclusion that we know all we need about our faith. Yet, we never stop growing and so, we should never stop learning. The goal of the Christian life is to learn to love as Jesus did. St. Paul calls the growth in love the "Fruit of the Spirit." He said that our lives will reflect growth as love, joy, peace, patience, kindness, goodness, gentleness, faithfulness and self-control become hallmarks of our lives.

It seems that we never effectively learn these lessons in isolation, so God sends us many teachers. Some are people that we might expect: religious figures, conference speakers, authors or mentors. Nevertheless, others teach what can never be found in books. They might not be the ones whom we would choose to open our minds, yet they are precisely the ones that God uses to teach us the lessons of the heart. Their ranks are legion. The person at work that I hate is, probably, one of these teachers, for God uses them to teach me patience and kindness. Anyone who "pushes my buttons" serves as a mirror of my inner life which waits to be healed. Instead of blaming the other for all that's wrong in my relationships or on the job, God uses others to show me my own frailty, lack of charity and unwillingness to live the Christ life. Parents, siblings or in-laws can teach forgiveness and compassion. Children teach that we have to give to another when we don't want to. Perhaps the men from the gardening service might be sent to teach us about diligent faithfulness in the midst of crushing circumstances. In other words, there are as many different teachers as people, and if we're smart, we'll learn from all of them.

The Dalai Lama calls the Chinese government that engulfed Tibet, "My Friend, the Enemy." When queried about this, he remarked that it was in the midst of the atrocities inflicted upon his people by the Communist oppressors that he perfected his practice of compassion. He said, "They've taken everything away from me, I couldn't let them take my peace of mind as well." This is a stunning testament to the power of the human person to learn and grow in the midst of the most dire of circumstances.

Like so much else in life, how we interact with others depends on perspective. You will encounter a variety of people today. Will you learn from them or be embittered by them?

Let the word of Christ dwell in you richly,
as in all wisdom you teach and admonish one another.
Colossians 3:16

Who irritates you the most, and
what is God trying to teach you through them?

16

Become Aware of Your Personal Drama

"Resolve to be thyself; and know that whoever finds himself, loses his misery."
Matthew Arnold

No one lives in a world isolated from others. While hermits pray in secluded monasteries, trappers hunt in the wilderness, and shut-ins languish in their homes, the very nature of human experience requires that at some point we relate to others. Those whose human contact is limited risk lapsing into a world of fantasy, memory or desire disconnected from lived experience. Home health workers report how clients overcome loneliness by reinventing loved ones in their imagination to be their companion. They set the table for them, talk with them during meals and sometimes argue with them incessantly. We all face the temptation to live by mental habits so strong that they can overwhelm our experience of life.

One purpose of the spiritual life is to come to consciousness, that is, to integrate our personality in a way that is healthy and balanced. A spirituality that denies human experience, with its ten thousand joys and ten thousand sorrows, is more a delusion than a path to God. Increasing awareness of ourselves and others, therefore, is both a practice of, and a goal of discipleship. In the 25th Chapter of St. Matthew's gospel, Jesus' strongest rebuke is for those who were so unaware that they failed to see him in the sick, hungry, naked, homeless or prisoner. Jesus not only censures the unrighteous for their inaction, but he reveals their blindness and hardness of heart as well.

One of the most profound obstacles to developing an open and loving awareness is our personal drama, that is, our habitual ways of relating to ourselves, the world and others. Instead of seeing people and circumstances as they are, we categorize them according to personal, familial and cultural values that we've made our own. If we do this regularly, these judgments become habitual and we place people somewhere within our personal hierarchy of meaning. Thus, the personal drama is born: complete with a cast of heroes, villains and supporting characters. Carl Jung once observed that we are at once, "the star of our own epic and a spear carrier in a greater drama." As with any good theater, we develop scripts worthy of an Oscar nomination to support our stories. People are either good or bad, based in large part, on how they make us feel. This is a response to what we perceive to be the overwhelming nature of life. If everyone has a role in the drama of our lives, then we find a degree of psychic comfort and security since we know what to expect and when to count on it.

Television soap operas are perhaps the most telling example of this mentality today. Scriptwriters design every word and action in a "soap" to elicit feeling. The hero sleeps with the vixen to irritate the ingénue, while the Senator embezzles from the campaign fund to support the illegitimate children. If we identify with the premise of the show, at its conclusion we feel vindicated, horrified or excited by what we saw. Besides being shallow, this is a very adolescent way of looking at the world. If you listen to the conversation of teenagers, it is chock full of "he said, she said" jargon. This is a telling characteristic of the insecure personality, for as we embrace maturity we learn to relate to people as they are, not as we need them to be. The habitual nature of our personal drama locks us into relationship patterns that deaden our soul and enslave us to routine. Since these habits reflect our inner life, the challenge is to become aware of and free from their snare.

Let us love not in word or speech but in deed and truth. 1 John 3: 18

Take a look at your personal drama. Who, besides yourself rates a starring role? Could they be different that you see them?

17

Celebrate with Abandon!

"Happiness hates the timid." Eugene O'Neil

A historian once said that the Puritans were afraid that somewhere, somehow, somebody was having fun. This attitude is a prevailing stereotype of the spiritual life. Many believe that to embrace the spiritual life is to shrivel up into a dry, boring husk of a person. As with any cliché, there is more than just a little justification for its longevity. Severity, wariness and a rejection of people are often the hallmarks of those who enter onto a spiritual path. The stories are legion of "normal" people who began religious practice and become a spoilsport. Let's set aside for a moment the obvious conclusion that people on the spiritual path threaten those who aren't. Given the dour countenance of many religious types, one wonders if they've ever heard that joy is supposed to be an outcome of the spiritual life.

Several factors may account for what has become the sullen spiritual path. First, some embrace spirituality as a refuge from addictive behavior. As such, their spirituality needs to give them a safe space to heal and reorder personal, psychic boundaries. This means, in practice, that they invest much energy in avoidance behaviors. The path to wholeness for the junkie, the sex addict, the compulsive spender or the gambler requires a clean break from harmful behavior. It makes sense, therefore, that their spiritual path has a measure of strong discipline to it. Couple this with the degree of self-hatred that addicts bring into recovery with them and it is not surprising that personal denigration often becomes part of the spiritual persona.

People who seek wholeness from addictions aren't the only ones who drape themselves in a mantle of hostility. All of us have been wounded during our lifetime, and these wounds ultimately become the scars which will alienate us from others. If our spiritual practice doesn't lead us to experiences of forgiveness and surrender, peace of mind eludes us and this shows on our faces and in our dispositions. This is common in American religion. Rather than undertake the liberating inner journey of conversion, many are content with outward semblances of spirituality which results in religiously miserable people. Others are afraid to show any sign of emotion because they don't want to be perceived as weak, so they remain frozen in stoic solitude. None of these experiences resonate with the freedom and joy of the disciple of Jesus.

The only effective antidote to sour spirituality is to drink deeply from the wellspring of celebration. Much of life is good and is ours to enjoy. God made us, like Zorba the Greek, to laugh, sing, and dance our way through life. We have the capacity to embrace others, enjoy good food, and take pleasure in the delights all around us. A healthy spiritual path encourages celebration with abandon, because it is our participation in the fullness of life.

Celebration is not to be confused with the superficial emotional excess so common in our culture. The attitude of "party 'till you drop" is the enemy of authentic celebration because it keeps us stranded on

the shoals of good feeling and particular circumstances. When we celebrate, we participate in God's joy for this world. Our singing, dancing,
shouting, embracing, and laughing bear witness that life is good, even
with its tender spots. We can go through life with a sullen spirit, but we
don't have to. Have fun-it's spiritual!

"Then the just will be glad; they will rejoice before God; they will celebrate
with great joy."
Psalm 68:4

Has it ever occurred to you that Celebration is a spiritual activity?
Can you teach your children the difference between authentic celebration
and the superficial license of popular culture?

18

Not Everyone is Going to Like You

"He makes no friend who never made a foe." Alfred, Lord Tennyson

It looks like the approval of others has become the emotional oxygen that we breathe. Ratings, polls, focus groups and market surveys all exist to tell those who wonder, what we feel. Cynical media commentators decry the practice of politics by poll results, that is, governance by popular opinion. Even the rare independent thinker in politics ignores the mood of the electorate at their own expense; for we've reduced sound bite politics to making the voters feel good about themselves. Some would even argue that the "blazing independent" is as calculated as the next politician, merely using incendiary rhetoric for partisan advantage.

For a long time, the media has exploited young people's social needs to sell products but, disturbingly, this tactic is working with adults as well. There was a time when only teenage magazines ran cover stories entitled, "How to make him like you!" Now, not only do women's magazines publish cover stories like, "How to get any man you want," but also testosterone-laden men's fitness magazines follow suit. From "How to turn heads when you walk into a room," to "Developing a body that women will die for," Madison Avenue's message is that one's popularity is the ultimate measure of a man.

Our current "cult of celebrity" is an example of this popularity ethic which deludes so many of us. A few years ago, someone must have told us that if we became famous, all of our troubles would be over. The athletic and entertainment worlds have certainly fostered this attitude, with maximum profit being rewarded for a relative amount of work. So now we bow at the altar of fame and celebrity without the slightest hesitation. The insatiable desire for fame has given birth to a new phenomenon in our culture: *celebrity for its own sake*. Those without sufficient moral strength or guidance literally do anything, from stripping on tabloid talk shows to shooting innocents from a car, to get noticed. The illusion in all of this is, of course, that some measure of celebrity or notoriety brings us acceptance and value. In other words, the lust for fame and attention is actually the archaic desire that resides in each of our hearts: we want to be loved.

In some ways, we as a culture have brought these neurotic impulses upon ourselves. Alice Miller established twenty years ago that when parents demand that a child meets their emotional needs, that child grows up with weak psychological boundaries. This leads in turn to youngsters who believe that their emotional well-being is rooted in the positive opinion of others. As a result, we have a generation of people who've grown up thinking that the most important thing in the world is to be accepted by other people. In colloquial parlance, this is "crazy-making," since no one is loved by everyone. Given the variety of temperaments, likes and dislikes in the communion of humanity, it is impossible for us to experience authentic affection and esteem, except from a few. So, to invest precious emotional energy trying to do the impossible is a waste of time and dignity.   Let's expose this insanity for what it is. Encourage your children to develop character, authenticity and purpose instead of seeking the adulation of others. Teach them that not everyone is going to like them, and that's okay.

Faithful are the wounds of a friend, and deceitful are the kisses of the enemy.
Proverbs 27:6

Do you even implicitly demand that your children exist to make you happy? Will you teach them to develop a few solid friendships and find their support there?

19

Open Your Heart and Do Something

"We cannot live only for ourselves.
A thousand fibers connect us with our fellow men." Herman Melville

From the east comes the story of a little parrot that lived in the forest with his friends the rabbit, the deer, the bugs, the badger and the snakes. One day as he flew home he saw to his dismay that the forest was on fire. He was horrified, because not only was he in danger, but also he knew his friends couldn't escape. In desperation, the little parrot flew to the closest lake, which was 100 miles away. He dipped his beak into the lake and then hurriedly flew back to the fire where he dropped his beak-full of water into the inferno. He then turned around, flew back to the lake, got some water, flew back to the fire and dropped the water. All day long, this valiant little parrot fought the fire alone. From the parrot's point of view, it didn't look like he was accomplishing much, be he knew that couldn't just let his friends die.

Higher up in the clouds, a majestic eagle watched the valiant parrot with some amusement. He flew alongside the harried little bird and asked him what he was doing. "My friends" the little parrot replied, "are in danger of burning up in that fire, so I have to put it out." "You simple little thing," the great eagle chided, "you can't put out a huge forest fire with your little beak-full of water. No matter how hard you try, you'll be lucky to save even one of them. You'd better just save yourself and get out of here." Never wavering in his pace, the parrot turned to the eagle and said, "Right now, I don't need your opinion. I need your help. If you won't help me, please leave me alone so I can save my friends."

In that moment the eagle's heart was broken. He was ashamed of his ridicule and saddened by his indifference to the needs of the animals in the fire. Unable to control himself, he began to weep huge eagle tears and resolved to help the little parrot. God and the angels in heaven were watching this drama unfold and were moved by the courage, love and compassion of the little parrot. They also began to weep, and so great were the tears which rained on the earth, that the deluge put the forest fire out and everyone was saved.

We can often become so overwhelmed by the needs of the world around us that we become numb to their urgency. Yet, I guarantee that there is at least one person in your life that is aflame and needs the cooling water of your love. All around us, people suffer from shame, humiliation, loneliness, poverty, despair, marital discord, abuse and addictions. The fire of these afflictions will eventually overwhelm them unless we decide that it's time to help.

We have enough love and resources to share with those who need us. But will we? After all it's easier to be an eagle and fly above the difficulties of life than to become a parrot that opens his heart to save the world. Each of us has been given the opportunity to do many things with our lives. We can squander our time and talent living out of an ethic of entertainment and consumption, or we can embrace selflessness as an act of commitment to those trapped in the fires of this world.

Heaven waits for the opening of your heart to join your efforts. Will you begin today?

No has greater love than this,
than to lay down one's life for one's friends.
John 15:13

Who in your world suffers today? Has your family ever seen you give to someone else without expecting something in return?
How do you expect them to learn what you won't teach?

20

Remember Who You Are

"A humble knowledge of oneself is a surer road to God than a deep searching of the sciences." Thomas a'Kempis

Anyone who uses a computer knows that when you turn it, there is a time where you sit there doing nothing while the computer comes "on-line." First, the power source connects with the computer to start the operating system which activates the hardware and loads software programs. Only when the computer has activated all of its various programs can you then get to work. The human person is much like a computer in the sense that we respond to life in ways that are both "hard" and "soft" wired. The archetypal elements common to all of us have been found in cultural motifs, stories, art and religions around the world. These common traits and characteristics are the hard wiring of our personality. We all have a common capacity for grief, joy, passion, despair and reverence. These shared traits express themselves differently in each person, but they exist in all of us.

On an individual level though, we relate to others through a combination of education, experience, and belief. These could be considered the soft-wired programming of our personal history. We are, in large part, a complex of our personal development, our family and cultural history which both define and restrict us. One way that we particularly identify ourselves is through the roles that we play in life. As men we live out of a variety of personas within a single day, sometimes even simultaneously! We are man, father, son, professional, laborer, athlete, musician, conservative, independent, progressive, religious, freethinker, alcoholic, addict, believer, sinner, Freudian and husband. Since our role-based identity, like the rest of our personality, doesn't develop in a social vacuum, we gather family and society's roles unto ourselves as well. Identifying ourselves as members of the majority or a minority, a "have" or "have-not," or part of the ruling or subordinate class provides a particular way to structure our personal energy and moral virtue.

This becomes, therefore, a pressing challenge, because our tendency to identify ourselves by the things we do is so profound that without our roles, we feel lost. Take a moment to examine all the various roles and functions that you play every day. Is there someone behind all of them? Are you so identified with fulfilling the expectations of being a father that you have little time to be a son? Are you so committed to your political ideology that you can't embrace someone who believes differently? Let's take the question a bit deeper: who are you when you aren't being "someone" or doing something? Is there anyone there behind the mask?

If you can't ever recall living apart from the expectations of some particular personal, tribal, or religious identification, then this is an invitation for you to begin the deeply personal journey of self-discovery. Living as a character in all the dramas of your world constricts your ability to respond wholeheartedly to life. There is more to any one of us than our roles allow us to express, for that is their nature: to direct our thoughts and behaviors. The spiritual life is replete with opportunities to peel away the layers of false identity until we discover our essential identity as a Son of God. Contemplation—the art of seeing what is—teaches us to look beyond the masks that we wear and to come to know the brilliance of God's presence within us. Like any life skill, contemplation is not caught, it's taught, and so we need to find those who will show us the way. But after reading this, if you're open, the teacher will come.

Who Do You Say That I Am? Matthew 16:15

Who are you when you're not busy doing something important?
Do your children know that there is someone behind your masks?

21

Pornography Is a Powerful Snare

*"The harmony between their hearts, their heads and sexuality is gone
and the pain of this loss is so deeply buried that they can't even recognize it."*
Jean Vanier

Imagine that you are standing on the top of a beautiful mountain, breathing in crisp, cool air as beautiful clouds pass overhead. Bask in the warmth of the sun and sense the well-being present in this moment of beauty and peace. And suddenly, by evil alchemy you find yourself trapped inside an enclosure so small that you are rendered immobile. Crystalline vision becomes shaded by shadow and illusion, and your freedom is cramped, distorted and diminished. Such is the experience of those who are trapped by addictions to pornography. We are created to enjoy beauty, pleasure and the satisfaction of union with others, but the vivifying gift of sexuality has become for many men, a prison of impotent passion and rage.

A survey of America's sexual landscape is not encouraging. There are literally hundreds of thousands of sites devoted to sexual expression on the Internet. In 1986 the Attorney General listed 2,325 magazine titles, 725 book titles and 2,370 film titles given over to sexual imagery, and that number has only increased in the past ten years. Yet, it's too easy to dismiss these as the perverted actions of a few who run to "dirty book" stores on the other side of town. The retail sale and rental of adult pornographic videos exceeded eight billion dollars last year, which was more that the total spent for regular box office movies. So we ask the question, why the deep fascination with pornographic fantasy? Why is sexual voyeurism, once disdained in popular culture rapidly becoming a mainstream past time?

It might be helpful to see the attachment to erotic voyeurism as an issue of psychosexual immaturity rather than as a commentary on sinfulness. The spiritual traditions of the world point to the illusory and sinful nature of pornography, and it demeans those who are caught in its grasp as either actor or observer. However, if we want to appreciate the pull of pornography on men, we need to understand the evolution of sexual maturity in the young person and those places it gets frustrated.

Sexual images are charged with raw emotional power. A young man, inexperienced in sexual expression can feel excitement and pleasure when exposed to pornography for the first time and it's easy for him to be drawn into this powerful world. Then, his fascination elicits both fantasy and vanity as he imagines himself an actor in the dramas spinning out before him. In other words, his voyeuristic impulse is rooted in an immature response to his emerging sexual drives for union with another. If someone helps him understand these powerful feelings and the temptation to displace them upon pornography, then his emotional development can continue unabated. He learns to integrate his sensual desires in a way that leads to authentic love in sexual relationships with real people. If not, a part of his personality will always be held captive to the "forbidden" images pulsating in his mind.

The shame that surrounds sexuality in America inhibits our ability to help young people when they need it the most. Instead of honest and compassionate instruction in one of the most important areas of a youngster's life, we either hide behind a mask of squeamish silence, or tell "war stories" of past romantic conquests. Our kids are at a crucial stage of their development. It's time that we grow up and help them.

When I became a man, I put aside childish things.
1 Corinthians 13:11b

Is any type of sexual voyeurism a challenge for you?
Is your sexual life integrated enough that you can help your son with his?

22

Habit is either the Best of Servants or the Worst of Masters

"The beginning of a habit is like an invisible thread, but every time we repeat the act we strengthen the strand, add to it another filament until in becomes a great cable and binds us irrevocably together, thought and act." Marden

Caution—life is habit forming! While a pun, this reflects something deeply true about life: we are often more ensnared by our habits than we think. Therefore, any reflection on the spiritual life profits by considering the role which habit plays in our relationships with God and others. Habits are those behaviors acquired by constant repetition which, in time, become either partially or completely involuntary. They provide us comfort, safety and constancy as they enable us to function on several levels of consciousness at once. If not for our capacity to form habits, we would have to learn to dress, tackle the subway, eat a meal, or mow the lawn afresh each day. When I was a Cadet at the Sheriff's Academy, my Drill Instructor was determined to teach me to keep my right-hand empty so I could pull my gun at a moment's notice. To this end, he decided that every time he caught me holding something in my hand, he would coat it with red spray paint. After several layers of paint, I became very aware of my right hand, and to this day, have difficulty carrying anything in it. Self-development programs are aware of this and offer techniques to lay unhelpful habits aside and develop new, supporting ones. So, habits can serve us profitably or run to the toxic end of conditioning and become addictions.

From a spiritual perspective, habits become impediments to growth when they dull our ability to respond creatively to God's daily invitation. Instead of the focused awareness necessary for spiritual growth, habit keeps us attached to behavior that is mind numbing. From the type of food and time we eat it, to the types of prayers we say, and the time of day that we say them, it is easy to spend our days on "automatic pilot," unaware of the divine presence within our life. One of the most fertile domains of habit is found in our thought patterns. Prejudice is but one example of habitual thinking that diminishes our ability to experience an authentic life. To prejudge someone based on any offensive category we've devised restricts our vision, stifles our hearts and traps us into a series of unloving responses that hurts everyone.

Habitual thinking isn't limited to prejudice; it's found in the ways that we respond to any of life's challenges. If our first impulse is to erupt into rage when conflict emerges, that is, in large part, a habitual response. Likewise, if we are manipulative, seductive, abrasive, reflective or vindictive in our dealings with others, these are habitual reactions programmed long ago. Eating when we're under stress or drinking when we're angry are habitual behaviors. And compulsive sexual activity is a habitual attempt to quench the loneliness of our souls. While this recounting of habitual responses could go on for several pages, it's sufficient to say that there is nothing like habit to close us off to God. Henry Van Dyke reminds us, "As long as habit and routine dictate the pattern of living, new dimensions of the soul will not emerge." If we spend our days in a cybernetic loop of unthinking habit, we dull our capacity for growth and life. Because of this, it's safe to say that first we make our habits, and then they make us.

"I have examined my ways and turned my steps to your decrees."
Psalm 119: 59

Where have your habits ensnared you today?
Wouldn't you rather be free?

23

God Gave You Power, Use It Wisely

"There is but one ultimate Power. This power is to each one what he is to it."
Ernest Holmes

There is something very good about being a man. We've been given strength, talent, wisdom, courage, humor, depth, passion and love. Men care deeply for families and friends, dedicate our best efforts to cure disease, build stunning civilizations and create breathtaking art. Yet there are some who don't appreciate the good that the masculine spirit brings to the world. You don't have to look far to discover anti-male attitudes in our culture today. Those exhibiting hostility toward men and things masculine run the gamut from feminist professors in universities to comics in night clubs, from politicians to Hollywood script writers. A Los Angeles Times article entitled, "Rape is all too thinkable for quite the normal sort of man"[6] is a good example of the attitude that sees men as more of a liability to the world than a benefit. "Misandry," the hatred of the masculine, now stands alongside "Misogyny" in the lexicon of gender politics and organizations exist to promote feminine dominance in the public and private arena.

This fear of masculinity is not without justification. While we are responsible for many technological, political and cultural advancements, so too, have we caused most of the horrors visited upon humanity. Patriarchy- the masculine interpretation of reality- has defined and confined women and minorities for hundreds of generations and this has taken its toll upon humanity. Jack Kornfield isn't far from the mark when he asserts, "war, ecological disaster and economic instability are literally *man-made problems*."

To admit this, however, doesn't lead to the assumption that men and masculine energy are intrinsically evil. Every monotheistic tradition of the world teaches that men, like women, are created in the image of God and are endowed with dignity and purpose. So, if men are innately good, why is it that we have brought great evil upon the world? The answer is simple: we have misused our power. We have taken our strength; creative energy and the ability to effect change, and dedicated them to the proliferation of our selfish agendas. History bears sad witness to the truth that when masculine power and unfettered consumption collide, horrific injury to others is the result. In our own century, dictators and despots have destroyed and enslaved millions through a misuse of their power. In other words, the problem was not that they were men, but that they were *evil men*. If an awakened, enlivening masculinity means any thing, it is that we have power to build, heal and restore the world. The task for our generation then, is to teach others that being a man means having power and that it can be good. We may use it for good or evil, but we cannot run away from it. It is a part of our destiny as a human being. If we refuse to acknowledge this power, it will wreak havoc, leading to depression, anxiety, and ultimately, rage. Richard Rohr puts it this way:

"The central masculine archetypes seem to always be about power: how is power good, how is power contained, how is power shared, how is power used for others, what is spiritual power and what is selfish power? We have show that maleness *is* about power, but power for good, power for others, power for life and creativity. "[7]

Until we come to the place where we are neither obsessed with nor terrified of power, we will remain small, fearful and violent men. When we embrace that which has been given us, we can work with women who are discovering their own dignity and power, to heal the world.

Yours is a princely power from the day of your birth.
Psalm 110:3

Have you made friends with power? Can you stand in your own power without bullying others or being afraid of them?

24

All You Need is Love

"I'll fight for you, I'll die for you, I'll lie for you, I'll cry for you. Everything I do,
I do for you."
"You are my heart and my soul, you are my destiny and my fantasy."
"I'm lost without your love..."Oh baby, baby."

If these lines sound familiar, perhaps it's because they are a parody of just about every love song on the radio today. If the "Top 10 Countdown" and romantic movies are your tutors, you'll believe that love is a bubbling expanse of tender, passionate feelings, as ethereal as the morning fog. According to culture, love is gained and lost in a heartbeat, based on a mood, a seductive glance, or a whim. We love to be overwhelmed with the feelings of desiring and being desired, just as we yearn to feel connected to beauty, strength and passion. And "falling in love" fits this bill very nicely. The world seems a softer and easier place to live in when we're immersed in the ocean of romance and passion. We hope that our "soul mate" will emerge from the shadows of life and take away our loneliness, pain and despair.

Yet, is that really love? If an alien came to Earth and looked at the state of our relationships, they'd conclude that whatever it is that we're looking for in love, we're not finding it! People come for counseling for a collapsing marriage who haven't celebrated their first anniversary, while couples preparing for marriage sign pre-nuptial contracts just in case the union doesn't "take." Maybe this is, in part, the consequence of looking at love through the eyes of pop chart ballads and tabloid bylines. When we think that love is only real when it is sensuous, thrilling, soothing and fun, then we set ourselves up for failure. So instead of mutuality and connection, we want our lovers to work some magic on us that takes away our loneliness and fear.

Many of us come to relationships with a whole in our soul so large that three partners couldn't fill it. Then, when the woman of our dreams turns about to be as wounded and incomplete as we are, we feel disappointed and even a bit betrayed. So, we move on and continue our search, looking for one, who in reality, will never be found. After all, our dream girl is that just that, a fantasy within us that we are hoping to project onto somebody "out there."

The search for the perfect women is a telling symptom of both our incomplete spiritual development and the degree to which we've fallen prey to a cultural mythology of love. When we expect that some woman will fulfill every fantasy, soothe every heartache and understand us as no one else, then disaster awaits. After all, aren't these the roles that mother should have played in the first years of our life? No woman can take away your pain, it's yours and you must heal it. No woman can meet every sensual fantasy that you ever have, but that doesn't mean that you can't love her with abandon anyway.

There are as many definitions of love as there are people trying to define it. For today though, let's define love as *the voluntary giving of myself for the good of another*, and not for my own satisfaction. Then, we can have a relationship with a woman which brings deep satisfaction on every level. Love isn't about seduction, fascination, obsession, or even getting my needs met. For if I'm only looking to get, then it's not love: it's just another act of consumerism. Love offers a lot, but only if you're ready to do the work to receive her.

Love never fails.
1 Corinthian's 13:8

Did anyone teach you how to love?
What do you want from love?
Can anyone meet your expectations?

25

Make Friends with Life's Seasons

"The world is not to be put in order, the world is order incarnate. It is for us to put ourselves in unison with this order." Henry Miller.

Until I moved to Western Pennsylvania to attend graduate school, I'd never lived through several cycles of the four seasons. Growing up in Southern California, I'd known sun, occasional rain, cool winters and smog. So, walking in the forests around Pittsburgh was a revelation for me. I saw the stunning beauty of autumn, bone chilling winters, vibrant spring colors and rainy, green summers for the first time. Learning to spot the way that nature unfolded according to seasons was both enlivening and instructive. It seemed that just as I became acclimated to one season and its particular design, then the next one was on its way. To make matters worse, it didn't matter if I was enjoying summer's heat or autumn's chill, when the season changed, it did so without my permission and I had to adjust.

It's easy to forget that life, like the weather, has its cycles, seasons and rhythms which are beyond our control. People who live in less affluent cultures understand this better than we do. It is almost as an article of faith for us that we can fix whatever is broken, refurbish whatever has been worn down, and replace whatever has worn out. Yet, life unfolds according to its rhythms, and we are powerless to change much of its course. From the life span of a virus to the duration of a drought, everything begins, exists and ends as a part of life's rhythms. Virility, strength, joy and renewal are as much a part of life as frailty, sadness, inadequacy and decay.

This reality is not limited to people and planets. It holds true for civilizations and cultures, as well. For thousands of years the Roman Civilization ruled the world in glory, but today is an archeological memory. Before Rome thrived, Alexander the Great conquered Persian kingdoms, which had overrun Egyptian empires that had destroyed reigning tribal kingdoms of the Near East.

So, in fact, nothing remains the same, including us. Our life will always be a mixture of praise, blame, gain, loss, honor, shame, joy, sadness, life and death. Disease comes and goes, difficulties rise and abate, and finally, we die. Desperate to control the uncontrollable, we run to the gymnasium, the hair salon and the plastic surgeon trying to snuff out any hint of ageing, change and death.

Native cultures embraced inevitable change of life as a part of the initiation of young men. In sacred rituals and stories of initiation, boys on the verge of manhood were told in no uncertain terms, *you are going to die*. This seems like a barbaric philosophy in the *"you can have it all"* age. But properly understood, this was good news. The young man learned that he was part of a world of change and limitation, so he was free to trust whatever came his way. Today we believe that life should only get better and we are easily irritated when it doesn't. So we come to see pain, loss and death as a betrayal of the divine plan, not a part of it. Recovery groups know that peace of mind comes from understanding which parts of life we can change and which we can't. They've taught us that most of our addictive behaviors are our response to the inevitable pain of life, and that sanity comes from resting in the limited nature of the world with all it's confusions and contradictions.

Without a solid understanding of the essential nature of change, we will ask more of life that it has to offer and be sadly disappointed when our illusions aren't fulfilled.

You are a puff of smoke that appears briefly and then disappears.
James 4:14

Are you known for fighting things that cannot be changed?

26

You Don't Get Away with Anything

"The fault, dear Brutus, is not in our stars, but in ourselves." Shakespeare

The world of self-development seminars is full of people who want to experience a happier, more prosperous life. Spending thousands of dollars each weekend, participants hope to learn strategies that lead toward satisfaction and hopefulness. These are worthwhile goals since they reflect the deepest yearnings of the human heart. After all, who doesn't want to be happy? I do! I want to be free from suffering, despair and frustration. I want to give my best effort to bring good things to me and those I love. I yearn to be free of the snares that encircle my heart and keep me trapped in self-defeating patterns. And like everyone, at times I need a mentor, one who has learned some of life's lessons, to point the way toward happiness and purpose.

Learning how to live a life that is satisfying, rich and meaningful is supposed to be an end of the spiritual life. Sadly, the Church is not always a place where we learn these lessons. When our faith community is reduced to moralistic proclamations, disconnected from living Spirit, we look elsewhere for the support and instruction we need to be happy people. But when we do connect with a spiritual teacher, one of the first lessons that we learn could be called "the principle of sowing and reaping." In other words, when we recognize that each action brings a result of some kind, then we are on the way to wisdom. This is really a wonderful commentary on the interconnectedness of creation. If I plant an apple seed, I'll have an apple tree. Likewise, if I fail to water the apple seed, the fledgling tree will die in due season.

The spiritual life teaches us that there is no disconnection between mind, heart and action at any point in our lives. Jesus told his disciples "Whatever a man sows, so shall he reap." If we imbue our relationships with enmity and ill will, we shouldn't be surprised when no one wants to be with us. Likewise, if patience, kindness and good humor are the seed-gifts we bring to life, then many will want to befriend us. Abuse drugs and you will suffer physical and mental consequences, eat food that's gone bad and you will get ill, stick your finger in the electric socket and you will be shocked. It's really this simple: every action brings a result.

Eastern religions call this process, "karma." In the Christian West, we have a hard time listening to any teaching on karma because it is often framed within a backdrop of reincarnation. Yet, one doesn't have to believe in eastern understandings of death and rebirth to understand karma that our actions have consequences.[8]

This reflection is offered to counter the notion that if we are good enough, beautiful enough, rich enough, or smart enough we can subvert the natural order of life. We eat as much as we want, as often as we want, and then marvel that we are the most obese nation on earth. We exploit other people and marvel at their resentment toward us. We surrender to every type of pleasure imaginable and can't understand why our soul languishes for meaning. We live in ways guaranteed to keep us miserable and are then depressed when a self-esteem workshop doesn't cure us. So, call is sowing and reaping, karma, or "whatever goes around, comes around," who we are today is the result of our thoughts and actions yesterday, and our efforts today will dictate the kind of person we will be tomorrow.

> *The scoundrel suffers the consequences of his ways,*
> *and the good man reaps the fruit of his path.*
> Proverbs 14: 14

Have you ever known a cause that did not bring an effect?
How can you teach your children the intersection of act and result?

27

Beware of the Other Man

"Own Your Shadow or It Will Own You." New Warrior Training Network

A man went to his family doctor with great back pain. Writhing in agony, the man lay on the examination table while his physician poked and prodded around. "Well, here's part of the problem," replied the doctor with astonishment. "You're laying on a backpack." The patient anguished, through gritted teeth, "I know, but I can't take it off It's connected to me." Much to the doctor's dismay, when he tried to remove the backpack, he found that it was tethered to the man's spine. So, he did the next best thing, he opened it up with the intent of removing its contents. Imagine his surprise when he looked into the bag and saw a gnarled, angry old man in the bag. When the doctor tried to take the little man out, he bit at him and hissed, "Keep away, he belongs to me!" The doctor closely observed this wizened little man and noticed that he greatly resembled his patient, except where the patient was fair; the man in the knapsack was ruddy. In fact, practically every aspect of his patient's appearance was manifested in just about the opposite way by the grouch in the pouch.

After his attempts at dislodging the intruder met with no success, the doctor took another tack: he decided to interview him and see if he could learn what would break him free. "So," asked the physician, "where did you come from?" Wheezing and rattling the pitiful little man pointed at the patient and replied, "I belong to him and, and he's mine." "I don't understand, what do you mean?" asked the doctor. "It's simple," he replied, "I was born the same day he was, only I never had the luxury of seeing the light of day." Sneering, he went on, "As he grew older, his parents told him that certain of his emotions and feelings were no good, so he tossed them into the back pack. I took them, and began to build my body with his discards." "Next," he continued, "when he went to school, his teachers and classmates ridiculed him for having feelings, thoughts and opinions. So, when he threw those away, I grabbed them and kept building myself a body." Quite pride fully, the troll went on, "Over the years he has taken just about every honest emotion, impulse or feeling that were his and he's tossed them away to make someone else happy." The doctor interrupted, "so you now have a complete body made of all his despised and rejected parts?" "You got it!" replied the gnome. "But wait," asked the doctor. "My patient is strong, successful and competent, but you are scrawny, deformed and, frankly, smell like hell. How can this be?" "It's simple really," he replied. "Your patient grew up in sunshine, fresh air and with lots of activity, but I've been shut away in this backpack made of his fear and self-loathing. He may have the limelight, but I'm the strong one who torments him. He has the looks, but I have the power."

Each of us has this *other man* to contend with. St. Paul knew him, Carl Jung called him the "Shadow" and even Thomas Merton lamented his presence in his life. Until we take the steps necessary to reclaim the emotions, insights and feelings that we've stuffed away, we will lack power, authenticity and purpose. Our lives crave the dynamic energy that we have an obligation to use for this beautiful, but broken world. Yet, until we befriend him, we will never know what riches await us. Get to know the other man today and let the mining process begin!

There is now no condemnation for those who are in Christ Jesus.
Romans 8:1

What does your *other man* look like?
If you take pride in your personal strength, you can count
on him being weak.
If you present yourself as pure, he will have a dark edge to him.
How can you keep your children in the light today?

28

You Will Die as You Have Lived

"We are what we repeatedly do." Aristotle

Remember the story that Jesus told of the quirky fellow who had so many riches that he decided to build larger storage barns, have a party and go to bed? In the parable, God appears to him in a vision and calls him to his eternal reward with a scathing rebuke for his foolishness. While the purpose of this parable was to point out the futility of finding security in riches, it also invites us to consider a principle of the spiritual life: we will die as we've lived. This comes as no surprise to those who work in hospice, pastoral or health care. Stories abound about people who die, as it were, "in character." We cannot spend every day of our lives filled with hatred, despair, envy and aversion and hope to die a serene death. The miser hoards every resource available from oxygen to bedpans as he completes his journey to the place of no possession. And people of deep faith die at peace, even in the midst of great pain and material want. If fear, judgment and self-loathing characterize the way a person has lived, the likelihood is that will be the way that they die.

Our life's patterns are in large part responsible for the way that we finally surrender to the end of life. Yet, this applies not only to our dying day, but also to every day. Our thoughts and actions lead to discernable, predictable patterns of behaviors. The vision of life that I've embraced and live out day to day, leads me to my destiny. Samuel Stiles reminds us, "Sow a thought, and you reap an act; Sow an act, and you reap a habit; Sow a habit, and you reap a character; Sow a character and you reap a destiny." In other words, if I'm committed to "looking out for number one" and fulfilling every sensual desire that I've ever had, then isolation and a feeling of spiritual dullness will be my companions. On the other hand, if I have decided to love God and the world with a sacrificial ecstasy, then serenity and joy will accompany me down the pathways of my life.

This is why it's so important to look deeply at the patterns of our life. Most of the time our approach to life is so automatic that it seems that we're flying on "automatic pilot." This may be helpful for cross country travel but it has deleterious effects on conscious living: not only do we lose the vibrant juice of a life vivified with the present moment, but we also strengthen life patterns which contribute to spiritual sluggishness.

So, as with other lessons in this book, we come back to the need for active and alert, contemplation. Will you risk taking the time to see where your life is caught up in some type of reactive living which dull your sensitivity and trap you in misery? Entering life with full attention directed to the "why's and how's" can actually be quite an overwhelming prospect. But every spiritual tradition of the world suggests that learning to look deeply and steadily at our lives is an essential step toward maturity. Do you want to live and die as you are today? Or, are you hoping for something a little more splendid? The choice is yours.

And do this because you know the time;
it is the hour now for you to awake from sleep.
Romans 13:11

What are the unwise patterns that you perpetuate in your life?
What have you passed on to your kids? Awareness or dimwittedness?
If it's the latter, then know that you're condemning them to misery.

29

You Remain a Victim Only if You Choose To

"If you permit your thoughts to remain on evil, you will become ugly."
Paramahansa Yogananda

Dr. Ian Smolitz died of heart failure in Manhattan at the age of 69. He was an amazing man, although he was certainly not famous in any sense of the word. Yet, to those whom he touched, he was clearly a man worth knowing. Dr. Smolitz was the only member of his family to survive the Holocaust. He endured the horror of the concentration camps and three times overcame death sentences. Nazi guards changed their minds about killing him twice because he was a doctor and they needed him in the camp. And once he exchanged his prison uniform and number with someone who had died from typhus, counting on the fact that the guards wouldn't get that close to check. Ian escaped captivity and helped, as part of the resistance movement, to liberate other camps at the end of the war. He immigrated to Israel where he won a medal as an army doctor and in 1957 came to the US where he taught, wrote about medicine and revamped radiology departments in three hospitals. He helped those who worked around him to aspire to a better station of life and he founded a program at Harlem Hospital to help local youths to become x-ray technicians. As the writer of the New York Times article that chronicled his life put it, "Dr. Ian Smolitz of Poland, Germany, Israel and Manhattan lived a life worth noting not because he survived a life of unimaginable horrors, but because he gave meaning and blessing to his survival."

Contrast this with the person who experiences inconvenience, calls it injury and sues, or one who suffered trauma decades ago, and yet insists on reliving it daily. Why is it that some can undergo debilitating trauma and come out of it with a degree of sanity and grace while others crumple up and refuse to keep living? Worse yet, why is it that some people actually cherish the wounds that life hands them and then insists that special gifts of beneficence be theirs at the expense of the common good? The self-styled victim is certainly not a new phenomenon, but it is one that has gained a political vibrancy in our age.

The spiritual path is more oriented toward healing victims than it is perpetuating "victim politics," but you'd never know it if you listen to some religious experts. Confusing political action with spiritual development, well-meaning people keep those who have been traumatized by life in dis-empowered social, moral or political roles which only serve to keep them victims. This is not in anyone's best interest.

In his landmark work with Holocaust survivors, Victor Frankl found that those who could find some sense of meaning and purpose, even in the midst of horror, were the ones who, like Dr. Smolitz could cope and provide blessing to the world. In other words, whether we let life crush us or not depends on our reference point. If we, like so many today, see ourselves as the center of our universe, then we'll have a hard time finding any way to make sense of the pain in our lives because our psyche isn't equipped to cope with crushing pain. On the other hand, if we believe that we live in relationship with God and others, then we have a

starting point for our suffering. The Christian can take comfort knowing that every facet of life has the possibility for meaning and purpose.
The message of redemption says that everything can be used by God to
teach, to reconcile and to restore. You may have been hurt terribly,
betrayed painfully and disappointed deeply, but the gospel says that
there is a way out. So if you choose to remain a victim, you may.

He bore our sins in his body on the Cross, that we might die to sin and live to
righteousness; for by his wound you were healed.
1 Peter 2: 24

Are you still at the mercy of those who hurt you?

30

Befriend a Truth-Speaker

"The best preservative to keep the mind in health is the faithful admonition of a friend." Francis Bacon

One of the best gifts we can give ourselves is to cultivate a relationship with at least one other man who will speak the truth to us, no matter what. In this world of confusing, and sometimes deliberate deception, we need men who perceive deeply and speak truthfully. This type of person isn't as readily available as you might think. Although men often pride themselves on "shooting from the hip" in conversation, the rivulets of illusion runs deep through our hearts and stain both our experience and understanding. It may be a sad part of the human condition, but as Alan Jones notes, we'd rather have the comfortable lie than the hard truth, because the hard truth runs the risk of breaking us open and exposing the darkness which we just as soon avoid.

The Truth-Speaker is one who assumes, at least in part, the role of the prophet for me. Nathan, the archetypal prophet of the Hebrew

Scriptures is a dazzling example of this rare creature. The story begins with the lustful yearnings of a Hebrew King. To cover up an illicit affair with a soldier's wife, King David manipulates battle assignments to kill her husband. When his plan works and Uriah falls in battle, David takes Bathsheba to himself and prepares for the birth of their ill-fated child. In the midst of daily court activity, Nathan barrels his way into the throne room and proclaims in front of everyone present that David is guilty of a terrible sin. Unlike the stereotype of the modern politician, David acknowledges his guilt and enters onto a path of redemption, which will cost him much humiliation and pain, but ultimately leads him to a graced peace of mind.

Archetypal psychologists tell us that the prophet is one who has accessed a characteristic of the "magician" archetype. This symbolic language points to the primary role of the truth-speaker: he brings the perspectives of heaven to the circumstances of earth. This is the same kind of language that Jesus uses when he promised his disciples that in his absence, God would send the Divine Spirit to lead them into all truth. Truth speaking, therefore, becomes the proclamation of sacred vision, for when we speak the truth, we see as God sees. This is, of course, why nobody really wants prophets around. The very expository quality of one who is committed to truth shines a bit too brightly in our personal and corporate darkness. So, instead of celebrating their goodness, we usually find a way to nullify both messenger and message. In contemporary history, names like Mahatma Gandhi, Oscar Romero and Martin Luther King resonate with chilly memory. These men went the way of profound prophets, to an early grave. But they are not alone. The history of the human race offers ample evidence to the fact that we don't want to hear the truth and we will ridicule, ostracize, imprison or liquidate those who are determined to tell it to us.

For men on the path of Spirit, seeking out and befriending a Truth-Speaker is actually an act of courage. To do so acknowledges that we have an almost unlimited capacity to fool ourselves and asks that another stand in the gap of honesty with us. Our personal prophets may, at times, be abrasive and sometimes, being human, may be wrong. But if we offer others the vulnerability of pointing out blind spots that we can't see, we will grow in wisdom and authenticity. Find someone today who will spot your hypocrisy and point it out to you, then hang onto them with everything you've got. Oh, and by the way, have the determination to become a Truth-Speaker yourself.

Faithful are the Wounds of a Friend, But Deceitful are the Kisses of an Enemy.

Proverbs 27:6

Is there anyone that you trust enough to tell you that you're wrong? Will you have the courage to embrace truth as a conscious act of your will?

31

Go on Your Vision Quest

"All the wonders you seek are within yourself." Sir Thomas Brown

My staff recently completed the arduous process of writing a Vision Statement. With ever increasing demands upon our time and resources we knew that we had to establish priorities and boundaries on our work. So we looked deeply at our desires, assumptions, prejudices and activities and built a filter through which we can examine and respond to all the ministry requests that come our way. While developing Vision Statements is on every corporate agenda, the spiritual life demands that we undertake a journey into the realm of Sacred Vision.

The Vision Quest, an intentional "going apart" from daily life to learn new ways of seeing, has become more popular recently, but the desire to look deeply has been constant from the advent of humanity. Temples, oratories, shrines, caves, churches, mosques, forest monasteries and sacred sites are a few of the places that the human has gone to seek divine vision. The desert, a symbol of death and rebirth, is a familiar image to Jewish and Christian mystics as the place one goes to hear the voice of God. The prophets of the Hebrew and Christian scriptures went to the desert, subsisting on next to nothing to await a vision from the Lord. Jesus follows this pattern and the gospel writers tell us that he experienced burden and bliss on his Vision Quest.

Yearning for a renewed encounter with God, I undertook a Vision Quest in the Wilderness of Canada. My experiences were truly marked with insights and visions, not so much of divine beatitude, but of my own brokenness and fear. Sitting inside my sacred circle for three days without food or water (in the pouring rain) literally brought out the worst in me. Every sound in the night became an occasion for terror, as I was sure that I was about to be eaten by a wolf or to fall victim to a bear. Anger passed through me in currents which then alternated with sadness, boredom, frustration and longing. It was in the rain sodden wilderness of Northern Canada that I saw myself as I really am, without the pretense of success and affluence. I wasn't priest, author, a speaker, dad, husband, or any of the other roles that I live in to keep myself sane. Instead, visions of shattered relationships, vitiated dreams and broken hearts poured forth from some deep part of me as I wailed into the thunder clouds looking for relief. But upon my return to the camp, I knew that I'd gained a sacred vision: that I was a man full of fear, a broken heart…and yet, good. Others came back to our group telling of conversations with animals, dreams of God, finding new freedom and insight. For me, however, my Vision Quest opened my heart to the pain and embarrassment that we all feel for the mess that we make of our lives.

So whether your Vision Quest produces ecstasy or agony, you must begin a pilgrimage of deep seeing. You already have a vision of life. It informs the way you relate to God and others whether you like it or not. The trick then is to discover what you hold to be true, precious and life giving and learning about your prejudices, hatreds and fears. For, to quote, Oliver Wendell Holmes, "Once your mind stretches to see something a new way, there's no going back." It is no accident that every religion asks its initiates to undertake some manner of the Vision Quest. Without it, you will remain hostage to the illusions of our culture and your experience. Go sit in a circle in the rain. You'll get more than wet.

Without a Vision, People Perish.
Proverbs 29:18

Have you ever been in a place where you couldn't hide behind your excuses?

32

The Mansion of "Yes" is Built Upon the Foundation of "No"

"The happiness of a man in this life does not consist in the absence of, but in the mastery of his passions." Alfred, Lord Tennyson

Here's a news flash: You can't have it all! Contrary to the lure of media and market, life imposes necessary limitations upon our energy. You cannot simultaneously be the President of the United States, a Catholic Bishop, soccer star, quantum physicist and a mom. You can't undertake a surgical residency in Minnesota while becoming a world-class surfer in California. Yet, if you listen to the jargon of self-improvement culture, a man who doesn't "grab the brass ring" every time it comes his way is a loser. According to these voices, to do without the best, the most lovely or stimulating is to have missed out on the purpose of life. The illusory nature of this, of course, is that the foundational premise is faulty. Spiritual traditions that have stood the test of time know what Jesus taught, that life does not consist in the abundance of possessions. While materialism isn't the only symptom of a malnourished soul, it is one of them. And interestingly enough, we can be as possessive of our family, careers, religious experience and love life as we are of things. Because in the end, our desire to "have it all" is a token of a broken heart yearning for healing.

None of this is to suggest that we don't have more potential for living a fully realized life than we do today. Actually the reverse is true; to live a life that enriches others and us requires a wholesale commitment to growth, challenge and a fresh and discriminating perspective. As we embark upon the adventure of our lives, we are faced with a myriad of opportunities. Some of them lead to success and fulfillment, others to desolation and ruin. The art of life becomes, therefore, the ability to skillfully embrace a path that opens our mind and heart to encountering life with our deepest energy. This is why every yes to life is necessarily bathed in a stream of no's.

The process of becoming physically fit is a good metaphor for our reflection. You cannot run a marathon race, become a world-class hurdler, a champion body builder or lose thirty-five pounds in one day. While you may be excited about the prospects of a newer, stronger body, the first few days of any fitness regimen is laced with soreness, muscle fatigue and doubt. Discipline and a graduated set of exercise over many weeks' leads to fitness. And along the way you must say "no" to many things that you have previously embraced for your "yes" to fitness to be effective. Hot fudge sundaes for breakfast? No! An ultra-super-gigantic burger, fries and milkshake? No! Lounging in bed instead of hours of exercise? No!

The same struggle between "yes" and "no" holds true for every area of our lives. If we want a wife, then "playing the field" gets a resounding no! An authentic prayer life requires that we set aside other worthwhile activities so we can immerse ourselves in God. Even writing the Great American Novel means that you type away while your friends swim, shoot pool and go to the movies. From a spiritual standpoint, boundaries and borders are actually quite good for the soul. They help channel our energy and slow down the rush of opportunity that drives us to distraction. This is the function in religious writing of the "Sacred No." We open ourselves to the possibility of the best by learning to say no to everything else, including the good. So today, let's take some time to teach our sons that life isn't cut-rate. Every possibility requires commitment, and all achievement is built upon purpose, priority and perception.

As God is faithful, our word to you is not "yes" and "no."
2 Corinthians 1: 18

Have you muddled the ability to say yes and no in your life?
Are you a model of clear, passionate, consistent effort for your family?

33

God's not Mad at You

"No man hates God without first hating himself." *Fulton J. Sheen*

If you watch television long enough, you'll see every religious philosophy under the sun broadcast for consumption. Last week I happened upon a show broadcast from Texas, which stirred up quite a bit of antipathy within me. The preacher's entire message was focused on faithfulness to God, something that I wholeheartedly endorse. The disturbing tenor of the program, though, was summed up in his conclusion: "Remember," the preacher warned, "If you don't worship the Most High God as my Bible tells you to, you belong to the devil and God has an eternity of fire, torment and pain for you and all the demons." What troubled me so much about this man's message was not his rather selective interpretation of scripture, as bad as that was, but rather the venom that he released onto the airways in God's name. According to the preacher, God is a wrathful, avenging deity, waiting to toss people into eternal torment for a violation of prescribed laws. Any suggestion that God is merciful, compassionate or tender didn't even register on the radar screen of this message. What this broadcast revealed to the discerning eye were three things: this preacher's likely image of God, his perspective on his parents, and his self-image.

Anyone in pastoral ministry encounters the collision of God image and self-image every day. People come to church, temple or mosque with an intrinsic expectation of who God is and how God relates to humanity. This God image colors our relationships to each other, frames our moral viewpoint and either supports or diminishes the amount of psychological energy that we have to face each day. If our God is the famous "absentee landlord" of the 18th Century deist, then we believe that God made us, but that we have to now fend for ourselves. If God is a deity who delights in punishing sinners, then we live on the neurotic edge, hoping to make it through the day without giving an offense likely to land us in hell. On the other hand, if God is wise, compassionate and just, we have the personal freedom to trust that we can grow, make mistakes, learn and move on, all the while secure in God's love.

Our image of God is a complex- like everything else in life- of our experience, temperament and education. A person who grew up in a loving home with parents who were wise, firm, tender and sympathetic will hold a very different conception of God than those who were abused or abandoned by their parents. Writing in the 1950's J.B. Phillips recognized this:

> "The early conception of God is almost invariably founded upon the child's idea of his father. If he is lucky enough to have a good father, this is all to the good, provided of course that the conception of God grows with the rest of the personality. But if the child is afraid of his own father, the chances are that his Father in Heaven will appear to him a fearful being...Many are

not able to outgrow the sense of guilt and fear, and in adult years are still obsessed with it, although it has actually nothing to do with their real relationship with the living God. It is nothing more than a parental hangover."[9]

Phillips accurately saw the co-relationship between parental, God and self-images. The task of Christian growth becomes the separation of the three. If I hate myself, I am likely to believe that God hates me as well. We need to plum the depths of our history and see if this is yet another unrealized relationship pattern waiting to be jettisoned for true gospel freedom. Jesus taught that God is not mad at humanity, sitting in heaven with a divine finger on the "destruct" button. Rather, Jesus showed us that God is like a wise father, a compassionate mother and a dedicated friend. So, if your God is still mad at you, it's not the God of Jesus.

No longer do I call you slaves...instead, I call you friends.
John 15:15

> **Who do you really worship? God or your parents?**

34

Be Willing to Lose Everything but Your Integrity

"If a man hasn't discovered what he's willing to die for, he isn't yet fit to live."
Martin Luther King, Jr.

In the 1960's, antiwar protestors often taunted police officers by calling them "pigs." Tiring of this, a creative policeman turned the insult into an acronym and, with the addition of three periods, the slanderous sneer of "pig" was transformed into a heartfelt recognition of "pride, integrity and guts" by the insulted. This slogan identified personality characteristics that resonate deep within the masculine psyche. Pride, and integrity and courage are values taught by athletics, military service, religious education and honorable family life. Like the virtues of pride and courage, integrity—the authentic expression of intention and action—has lost a measure of value today.

Part of the crisis of modern masculinity is found in the loss of men's integrity. We have traded clarity and power of our soul for cheap advantage in this era where the only thing that matters is "success." By sacrificing our integrity upon the altar of expediency we place families, our communities and ourselves at risk because we have lost our ability to stand for anything of value. By living a life that is fraught with compromise and duplicity we proclaim that we value little and are willing to defend even less.

The erosion of integrity has not happened as the direct result of a frontal assault upon virtue so much as by an increasing loss of our sense of the sacred. Integrity connotes completeness, wholeness and interdependence within a person. To be integrated means to be in a state of proper relatedness to myself and others. What is the evidence of vibrant spirituality but a state of harmony, clarity and direction that lead to the unification of thought, word and action?

Without integrity, we are scattered about by the winds of every prevailing force that catches hold of our psychic sails. It seems that popular culture thrives on the duplicity of the human heart. We celebrate the death of committed relationships in soap operas, applaud the "every man for himself" attitude of professional athletes and try to find excuses to disregard anyone who disagrees with us.

This reflection on integrity is not merely a call to a moralistic way of life. What I'm asking each of us to consider is the possibility that *there is a way of life that gives as much as it demands.* To be a man of integrity requires that we live a life of consummate standards and impeccable action…that our word indeed becomes our bond. While it is true that the nobility and beauty of an integrated life holds us accountable for our actions, stability, peace of mind and joy are its effect.

A motivational poster that I saw in a store the other day put it well: "Integrity is one of several paths. It distinguishes itself from the others because it is the right path, and the only one upon which you will never get lost." Imagine the peace of mind that comes at the end of each day knowing that you lived out of the wellspring of integrity, having nothing to hide, to be afraid or ashamed of.

The world needs men who have walked the path of discipline, healing and awareness, which leads to deep personal integration. For too long, our fractured lives have been evident for all to see. Our deepest desires to live with rich meaning have been frustrated by our duplicity and only a return to rigorous integrity will open the way for us to live as men of authenticity and spirit.

Is not your piety a source of confidence, and your integrity of life your hope?

Job 4:6

> Where do you "hedge your bets" and live outside the nobility of integrity?

35

Glory or Misery: Your Choice

"The Glory of God is Man Fully Alive." St. Irenaeus

It is true that men live lives of quiet desperation. The drumbeat of our heart is muted by necessary obligations of family, the strictures of our careers and dulled by bad habits that we've acquired over the years. Our culture wants tame men who are willing to fit into the easily controlled straight jacket of societal expectations and enslaved to the acquisition of wealth as the only evidence of their vitality. Men who dare to live outside this "ethic" find themselves marginalized and even ridiculed. Notions of heroism and nobility can evoke insult as much as admiration in people today. Our souls wither because we are not taught how to, or are expected to live with passion and purpose. These forces take their toll on us. Men suffer from addictions to drugs, sex, alcohol, excitement and work in a much higher proportion than women and we get sicker, and die sooner as well.

Part of our common cultural mythology is that men are supposed to be "good boys," lead a quiet existence and when we retire, turn into golf-playing, doddering old fools. This runs contrary to both the evidence of great cultures and our own inner inklings. Men can live with passion, contribute greatly, and grow older with wisdom, dignity and majesty. The fact that other cultures revere their elders has been so often stated that it runs the risk of becoming a stereotype. But it's true, a life dedicated to growth, love and service doesn't end when you turn sixty-five.

It's time to recognize that we have surrendered the deepest and richest purposes of our lives for the pitiful portion of approval. Our soul has withered and our neuroses point their gnarled fingers back at us as glaring witnesses of our surrender to common illusions. While we hear from religion about a state of grace, it is also true that men were created to live in a state of glory and to burn with deep flames of love, passion and service. Our heritage as sons of God is one of magnificent glory by which we are to illuminate this shadow-bound world. Gabriel Maurens once said, "The minute you stop burning with love is the minute that others begin to die from the cold."

Our desires are not evil and our passions are not destructive unless we keep them trapped within an adolescent mentality, which sees them only as means for self-satisfaction. The hunger for love that burns deeply within you is God waiting to break out afresh into the world. The anger that smolders just under your breastplate is the voice of justice that infuses your soul. And the yearnings for celebration and a good time are the seeds of God's ecstatic passion ripening to fruition for the banquet of the kingdom. Understand that these desires are the essential elements of your path to glorious love and service.

The ancient ones knew that to lives gloriously was to reflect God's glory. As such, all glory is reflective: it comes out of our sharing in God's life and purpose. But until we are taught how to tap into the deepest parts of our soul and burn with God's passion, we will remain depressed, angry little boys in men's bodies. D. H. Lawrence hints at this when he writes:

> Men should group themselves into a new order of sun-men. Each turning his own breast straight to the sun of suns in the center of all things, and from his own little inward sun nodding to the great one. And receiving from the great one his strength and promptings and refusing the pettifogging promptings of human weakness.[10]

Let us resolve today to live as men of brilliant glory and passion!
"My glory is fresh within me, and my bow is renewed in my hand!" Job 29:20

Where will you find glory today?
Whose opinion keeps you cold and afraid?

36

Everything Belongs

"If you can't fight, and you can't flee, flow." Robert Eliot

Having just returned with 10 boys from the Wilderness of Canada, I encountered a lesson that is both uncomfortable and reassuring simultaneously: everything we encounter in life belongs there. In other words, every circumstance, conflict, joy or sorrow has the potential to teach, lead, heal, correct, inspire, or bless us. At the end of a trip replete with insects, rain, portage challenges, and strenuous canoeing, one of the elder men reminded us of the facts of life in a canoe. He said that while in the wilderness you have a 95% chance that it will be too hot, too cold, too humid, too dry, or too buggy, and that 20 minutes later, it will all change and then be too hot, too dry, too humid, or too buggy.

The gift of the wilderness is one that we hide from in our technological society. When rain pummels, or the sun blazes and the wind threatens to capsize your canoe, it does so without your permission. So, you discover two ways to respond to the "catastrophe of the moment." You become a victim of nature and huddle up, miserable in your tent, until the unseemly weather changes, or you pray for the wisdom to understand

115

what the Spirit is revealing about to you. Perhaps what you learn is that you are easily afraid of being overpowered by forces stronger than yourself. Or maybe you learn that what you want more than anything in the world is not challenge and hearty fellowship of other men, but the comfort of a warm and feminine environment. In the wild you learn that everything belongs, including your responses to nature's encounter with you. David Knudsen, the Director of the Northwaters Program puts it this way:

> We have learned that the wilderness helps people get over thinking that they are victims. We tell them, 'When you're canoeing and it's raining, you can make the next hour miserable, or you can make it wonderful. It really doesn't have much to do with the weather. The solution is in the conversation that you are having with yourself."[11]

This is a truth of human experience: we respond to the challenges of nature in the same way we respond to every challenge in our lives. If we run for cover every time something unpleasant comes in the wild, we will do the same when the boss becomes demanding. If we let a pesky yellow jacket disturb us, it's likely that any obnoxious person can distract you as well.

Understanding that "everything belongs" is a direct route to sanity and it gives us a way to deal with the inevitable pain of life. All of our experiences are laced with joy, sadness, challenge, comfort, pain, humor, sensuality and tedium. Our first response to them is usually to accept what we like and discard the rest. While this seems like the most logical thing to do, it's actually a bit crazy making, because in case you hadn't noticed, life refuses to be discarded. AIDS is here, cancer doesn't want to leave, families rupture and tornados destroy entire communities. Our flight from life will inevitably isolate us from God and others. But when we see that everything is part of life's curriculum then we are plunged into mystery where we finally understand that we are not God.

It takes courage to embrace life, but the spiritual path reminds us that we don't journey alone. Everything that we face, no matter how painful, has the seeds of restoration, renewal and reconciliation within them. Until we can open our hearts and acknowledge life's incessant presence we can never truly be integrated men.

All things work together for good to those who love God and
are called according to his purposes. Romans 8:29

What painful or frustrating experiences are you keeping at arms length today?
Have you considered that they hold the key to a life that you only dream about?

37

Take a Stand FOR Something!

"You will become as small as your controlling desire;
and as great as your dominant aspiration." James Allen

Perhaps the most difficult conversion for a person on the spiritual path is to move away from the negative energy that envelops us and to embrace a positive view of life. We live in an era dominated by being "against" people and things. In the political arena, it seems as if we'd just as soon present a negative visions, complete with an evil cast of characters as offer a positive, uplifting one. Besides being an effective electoral tactic, the politics of resentment offers a made-for-sound-bite way of approaching life: not too many questions or deep thinking required. In other words, when I am "against" you, I have a way to feel good about myself. It's as though we have so precious little personal or corporate identity that we have to steal the shadow of one from those with whom we disagree.

"That's only in politics," we might say, hoping that our spiritual institutions show another way. Sadly though, religious America doesn't offer as many alternatives to this "demonization of the other" as we might want. In communities where people identify themselves as followers of the one who commanded unconditional love, there are too many examples of a religion of alienation. Jesus said that his disciples we were to be known by the uncompromising love of brother and sister. Instead, Christianity often becomes synonymous with intolerance and negativity. In church on any given Sunday, conservatives hate liberals, who ridicule traditionalists, who dissociate themselves from everyone else, because everyone else is going to hell.

When we define ourselves by what we are against, rather than what we are for, we limit our ability to see new ways of living and to enjoy ourselves. Negative energy poisons the well of our family, friends or community and medical research shows us that negativity even places our health at risk. Physicians know that a loving, positive attitude releases chemicals throughout our bodies that enhance our immune system and repel disease. We also know that pessimism and despair triggers the release of chemicals, which decrease our ability to withstand disease. It's as though there is a subtle valve within our spirit that loosens either a healing or toxic presence depending on our state of mind.

Contrary to much religious teaching today, we must remember that *a faith-filled vision is essentially a positive one.* Without an enthusiasm borne of the Spirit we languish in a whirlpool of negativity, dragging countless companions down with us. The ancients saw enthusiasm as evidence of God's life (*en-theos…God within*) and positive vision fuels our heart and mind with goodness and joy.

The state of the world presents us with many wrongs to make right. Around the world people are abused, exploited and marginalized. Our duty is to give of our most generous impulses to correct the injustices of our time, but we cannot effectively do good if our predisposition is a negative one. This means that we accept God's positive vision *for* life, *for* holiness, *for* drug-free youth, *for* strong families, *for* safe communities. Don't fall into the trap of being against much; there are too many challenges that await your positive energy.

> *Do not be overcome by evil, but overcome evil with good.*
> *Romans 12:21*

If someone were to write your obituary today, would they describe you as positive and faith-filled, or a monger of negativity?
Count the insults and barbs that come from you.
You'll be surprised at the insidious nature of your negativity.

38

Kindness is a Masculine Virtue

"Three things in human life are important: The first is to be kind. The second is to be kind. The Third is to be kind." Henry James

Masculinity has a certain steely edge about it. If a group of people tries to define what makes "a man, a man," traits like assertiveness, resolve, a toughness and passion commonly tops the list. We expect a man to be rough and tough, and we're almost disappointed when he's not. Perhaps this is because our culture still idolizes the tough-guy. John Wayne, Clint Eastwood, Steven Segal and others perpetuate the impression that the "real man" kills the enemy, "has" the woman and rides off in splendid solitude until it's time to save the world again. Professional athletics, most notably football and ice hockey, has a warrior-like quality, which enshrines an aggressive masculinity and lends credence to the notion that to be a man is to be "hard." Sam Keen puts it this way:

> "Men and women alike constantly exhort little boys to "act like a man," to be muy macho, a big man, a real man, an alpha male. Men live under constant dread of being labeled a sissy, a weakling, a wimp or a queer."[12]

121

It's important for us to recognize that the steel that fortifies the masculine heart can be a good and holy thing. Archetypal psychologists have done us a great service by uncovering the connection between masculinity and what they've identified as "warrior energy." They tell us that within men's psyche is the capacity and energy for serious, passionate, committed action, even in the face of grave difficulty. It is this energy that gives a man the ability to battle darkness without counting the cost and to sacrifice his life in pursuit of a noble cause. It is the spirit of the knight, the solider, the policeman, the protective father and the social activist. The energy of the warrior in its holiest form gave Martin Luther King, Archbishop Oscar Romero and Mahatma Gandhi the ability to withstand danger and controversy to work for peace and goodness.

Which brings us to the point of this week's reflection: kindness is a masculine virtue. For too long kindness, simple humane goodness has been viewed as a sign of weakness in the masculine world. This is in part due to a threadbare view of manliness that still haunts us. No sense of grace or kindness is possible and one risks being labeled and rejected by his peers for being benevolent and tenderhearted.

Fortunately this darkness of thought always wilts in the presence of kind and powerful men. These profound ones have always been with us, but it's just that we've preferred to confuse power with heartlessness. Jesus turned this notion upside down in the gospels. Power, he told us, was always to be found in the exercise of service, not in "lordship." So, it is the kind man who is truly the powerful man. If you run into a man whose heart radiates kindness, you can sense that is he is a different kind of being. First, he is not possessed by anger. This man has known his share of pain and sorrow, but has walked the journey of forgiveness and is at peace with himself and others. Having tasted of the fullness of life, with all of its joys and sorrows, the kind man also knows the experience of grace. He is aware that there is a Spirit within that is always enlarging his heart and freeing him to be more loving. As such, the kind man has embraced compassion. He knows that we all have been wounded by life and hopes that we can experience the grace, forgiveness and love that healed him so. Ultimately the kind man is a gospel man, one from whom the Spirit of God radiates like ten thousand suns. The world needs you to be such a man.

The fruit of the Spirit is love, joy, peace, patience, kindness, gentleness, goodness, faithfulness and self-control.
Galatians 5:28.

When was the last time you prayed, "Lord, make me a kind and gentle man? Will you have the courage to pray that today?

39

You Are Your Brothers Keeper

"What do we live for if not to make life less difficult for each other?" George Eliot

If you tune in to talk shows across the country, you'll hear people speaking with great passion about "biblical lifestyles" nowadays. It's no wonder. The past thirty years have seen the growth of popular opinion and scholarly theses that suggests that there is no particularly "right" way to live. "What is good for you, may not work for me," says the free thinker with a hint of pitiful self-righteousness. While some of what the social dissenter says is true, much of it is illusory. Our culture bears the scars of a self-indulgent era where divorce is assumed and children are increasingly left to fend for themselves. So, talk show guests thunder about a return to biblical morality, which looks quite a bit like 1950's Middle America. Prophets of the airwaves put their nostalgic yearnings in religious plastic-wrap and exhort listeners to support a return to "traditional values." Usually they mean a return to ethical and moral practices that have under girded culture for the past few hundred years: chiefly a return to two parent families, premarital chastity and monogamous heterosexuality.

Conspicuously absent from these exhortations on spiritual morality, though, is any concept of caring for those less fortunate than ourselves. We are hard pressed to find any television evangelist who pounds his fist on the pulpit and begs us to send our money to the urban poor. Yet, an honest review of both the Hebrew and Christian scriptures reminds us that the poor have a place of favor at God's banquet table. When we're confronted with passages that command generosity as evidence of discipleship, we spiritualize them, much as the Pharisees did in Jesus time.[13]

It is so hard for successful Americans to accept the notion that we have any responsibility for the poor in our communities. Why, that's almost un-American! After all, the hero of the American mythology is the man who scratched and sweated his way to the top. We have little time or sympathy for those who fail in the game of life and if left unchallenged by the Gospel, such attitudes quickly turn into resentment. After all, there are poor who take advantage of our generosity and lazy people who would just as soon live on the dole as work. So we feel justified in closing our heart and hoarding our wealth. Sadly, in a world where thousands starve to death each day, this sentiment is held by many who would otherwise claim to be fervent disciples of Jesus Christ. Of course, money really isn't the issue. What matters is that the way we use money speaks volumes about our inner life: are we people of generosity or do we have a miserly spirit?

Ultimately our relationship to the poor hinges upon our understanding of stewardship. If we truly believe that all we have is from God, then our responsibility is to manage our resources faithfully. And this would include a biblically inspired generosity toward the poor. On the other hand, if we think that our wealth is exclusively the result of our hard-earned efforts, then we will not give anything away easily. A national radio talk show host said last year that nobody had the right to tell him what to do with his money. This is true only if we choose to live disconnected from spiritual intuition. A gospel vision, however, invites us to see God reflected in the eyes of the poor and asks that we bless him there with kindness and generosity. The Scriptures are clear though: reject the poor and we reject God, bless the poor and God will bless us. Men of generosity, men of compassion. Now there's a biblical lifestyle worth embracing!

"Truly I say to you, whatever you do to the least of my brothers and sisters, you do to me"
Matthew 25: 40

Has your family ever witnessed you opening your heart to the poor? Will you teach them that to bless the poor is as fundamental an act of Christian Discipleship as going to church?

40

You Are Blessed to be a Blessing

"The best effect of a fine person is felt after we have left their presence." Emerson

Deep within a man's heart lies a dormant power that can change his life and bring an abundant vitality to the world. Precious few know of its existence and even fewer believe that we can use it in the lives of those we love. What is this life force? It is the ancient power of blessing. Every man can bless others by his words and actions, and our world withers because we don't.

As a culture we don't understand what is means to bless another. Either we reduce a blessing to a social catchphrase, such as *"God Bless You"* at every sneeze, or we relegate it to some religious "thing" that ministers "do." *"Give me your blessing"* becomes *"Give me your permission,"* and we utter a sympathetic, *"Bless your heart"* when someone shares their troubles with us. Yet, is there something more to blessing each other than semantic propriety?

Properly understood, to bless someone is to intentionally accept, validate and encourage them. The Hebrew and Christian Scriptures offer different types of blessings, but ultimately a blessing bestows positive energy, good will and invokes divine love upon another. In their book "The Blessing," Gary Smalley and John Trent suggests that a blessing has five components to it. Each blessing, they say, includes a meaningful touch, a spoken message, attaching high value to the one being blessed, picturing a special future for the one being blessed and an active commitment to fulfill the blessing.

Historically, kings and gods dispensed blessings to their subjects. In antiquity, when a king blessed you, you shared not only in his favor, but also his life energy. So it was important to make a pilgrimage where God, or the king would see you and in his seeing you, bless you. This notion continues down to our day through royal audiences, papal visitations and even in an immature way, by the swooning of young girls in the presence of celebrities. Royalty and deities were not the only ones who blessed others though. Patriarchs blessed their families, prophets blessed their governments and apostles blessed their disciples. Whatever its form, the blessing of another was a gift of favor, security and validation.

Our generation is blessing-starved. Men and women carry a dull, but persistent ache inside as they go from relationship to relationship looking for someone to affirm them, to tell them that they are good enough. For many, our childhood homes, the place where blessings should have been showered upon us, became the arena of curse and insult. Instead of affirmations, our memories echo with litanies of *"You're no good,* *""Why can't you be more like him?"* and *"You'll never amount to anything!"* From our parents we received either a sense of personal well-being and security, or a self-image with which we struggle until grow into emotional adulthood.

The words that come out of your mouth have the power to build people up or tear them down. If you want to, you can become a man of blessing, like the king of old, who looks for the good in people and affirms that at every opportunity. You can take your child into your arms and watch them blossom as you tell them that you love them, believe in them and dedicate yourself to their welfare. Bless your family and friends and watch them come to life. As with everything else in the spiritual life, what you give to others will be returned to you. So, become a blessing and become the blessed!

It is a blessing I have been given to pronounce; a blessing which I cannot restrain.
Numbers 23:20

Do you find that your words are a blessing to those you love or a curse?
Your words will have a lasting impact on your children.

41

Change Your Center of Gravity

"We have grasped the mystery of the atom and rejected the Sermon on the Mount."
Omar Bradley

What is the difference between those holy people that we call saints and the rest of us? Chiefly it would appear that they've learned that the purpose of their life is not to please themselves, but to do God's will. In other words, the focus of their psychic energy has been transformed from self-gratification to love and the service of others. We would be hard pressed to find a person with any measure of personal and spiritual authenticity who hasn't undergone a journey of metamorphosis. Like the butterfly, the holy person has, either by their own choice or through the vicissitudes of life, died to the allures of the ego and embraced love as the primary motivation of their existence.

This invitation to transformation is at the heart of the Christian message, but it isn't unique to western religion. The message that "life isn't about you" is a lesson of masculine initiation that aboriginal people have taught their young for generations. It looks like more "primitive people" knew that unlimited expectation leads to an absolute inability to form community. So it was important that the young man knew in his heart that he was not a solitary individual, but a member of what Alan Jones calls the "commonwealth of community."

Admittedly, in our "have it your way" culture, a message of love and service can fall on deaf ears. Our affluence and technology make it easy for us to fall into the trap of entitlement, that is, thinking that just because something exists, we have the right to it. In our consumer society, it is imperative that we embrace *entitlemania* as a common ethic otherwise we might balk at spending $250.00 for a pair of sneakers. The spiritual path points out, however, that the feeling of entitlement is really another mask of the fallen, wounded person who is looking for meaning in their lives. Just as the bully is actually a coward in disguise, so too is *entitlemania* a smokescreen for a hollow soul.

Since we comprise only 20% of the world's population but consume 80% of its goods, there is a particular urgency in finding the antidote for the empty heart. The rate that we consume "things" in an attempt to assuage our personal and corporate emptiness is a scandal to the rest of the world. We point to our Christian heritage with pride while one celebrity makes more to endorse athletic gear than the entire third world factory does to produce it and we spend more in video games in one year than most families in the developing world can earn to feed their families. Are we to think that Jesus doesn't care that we live in even relative opulence while the rest of the world starves?

The only remedy for the impoverished soul is to walk the journey from self-gratification to self-transcendence. If we think that life is about us, our needs, our desire, our delicacies and our tastes, we will remain miserable. Like the saints, we must discover that a relationship of love and rooted in service to God and humankind is what satisfies our thirst for meaning and purpose. Albert Schewitzer once said to his students, "I don't know what your destiny will be, but one thing I know: the only ones among you who will be truly happy are those who will have sought and found how to serve."

Whoever wishes to become great must become a servant and
whoever wishes the first place must become the servant of all.
Matthew 20: 26-27.

> **When no one is looking, answer this question...Who do you really live for?**
> **Is it making you happy?**

42

Fill in the Blanks

"It is dangerous to go into eternity with possibilities which you have prevented from becoming realities.
A possibility is a hint from God. We must follow it." Soren Kierkegaard

People don't seem to appreciate puzzles like they used to. Perhaps in our fast-paced society sitting down to put a puzzle together takes too much time. Some still love the challenge of facing a tabletop where thousands of pieces sit in a jumbled heap waiting to be assembled. I don't have much patience for a fresh puzzle though. I do become quite an expert when it's about four pieces from being completed. Then, I sit back and view the beautiful panorama of my efforts, just in time for someone usually to come along and knock the table over.

The spiritual life has been likened to a puzzle. We approach the disorganized piles of our energy, philosophy and experience and begin the ambitious adventure of putting all of it together in a way that is holistic and loving. Admittedly, we run the risk of stretching the comparison of puzzles and the spiritual life too far. After all, the work-in-progress of our relationship to God and each other is never complete. I always have more to learn, more to let go of and more to embrace. But in those moments when I am more loving, more holy, or more devoted then I know that the journey is worth the fare.

Spiritual directors tell us that the modern word for putting the puzzle of our lives together is "integration." Modern man is disintegrated, thanks in large part to our fractured society where there is little, if any, relationship between our spiritual impulses and the rest of our existence. Scientific advances have tried to disconnect our minds from our bodies, and moral life is reduced to individual preference, divorced from any standard of religious impetus. Antidepressants are the most consistently prescribed drugs in America and heart attacks occur like clockwork while we bloody our way up the corporate ladder.

What's a modern man to do? Is there a way to "pull it all together? Where are all the kings' horses and all the kings men when I need them? Psychology alone might not be the answer: people have been in therapy for years now with little to show for it. And religion is sometimes as much a part of the problem as it is the answer. Instead of helping us rebuild or restore our lives, institutional religion gets caught up in lifeless arguments and name calling which drives people away from the Church in droves.

What we need is a path of integration that brings every part of life into a holy symmetry, uniting passion and intellect, action and reflection. In other words, we need to find a way to fill in the blanks, to take those places where we've been afraid to grow, and to blossom. Perhaps we're reticent to express ourselves emotionally. Until we do, we will remain an intellectual husk of our true selves. Or maybe becoming vulnerable and trusting another is a frightening prospect. Yet, trust we must! This is particularly difficult for men who value competence and control. But until we begin to experience a deepening of our soul we will remain scattered, off-balance and neurotic.

It is impossible to make this journey of integration alone. So find other men who will share this process with you. They are out there, and want to grow as much as you do. Otherwise, you will remain cold, sterile and lonely.

> "Repairer of the breach," they shall call you,
> "Restorer of ruined homesteads."
> Isaiah 58:12

Where are there missing blanks in your life?
Do you have someone who will walk the journey of integration with you?

43

Don't Quit!

"Nothing splendid has ever been achieved except by those who dared believe that something inside them was superior to circumstance." Bruce Barton

For all of his graciousness in the New Testament, it appears that Jesus didn't have much tolerance for false starts. To him, authentic living had an "all or nothing" quality to it. The dead were left to bury themselves, a hand put to the plough was not to turn back and a campaign was not launched without a thorough cost analysis. He knew that nothing great was ever accomplished by half-hearted efforts or casual commitments, which is of course, terrifies the modern era. We want it all, thank you very much, but at a bargain basement rate. Marriage is temporary, children are valuable if they don't get in the way and the only thing we dedicate ourselves to with an insatiability of spirit is making money.

All this suggests that we would be well served to take another look at the gospel virtues of perseverance and faithfulness. Once rooted deeply in the soil of our lives, the ability to remain committed to a task, no matter the cost, bears great fruit. While it's not easy to always live out, the lesson is actually quite simple: don't quit…that's it. Once you make a commitment, see it through to the end. Don't let fatigue; fear, apathy, anger, sadness, difficulty or the opinions of others nudge you off the path of fidelity that you've begun.

One of my favorite musical productions is the "Man of La Mancha." Its hero, Don Quixote de la Mancha, suffers from weak mindedness and lapses into fantasy where every windmill is an opponent, every stable maid a princess, and his life a noble defense of God and virtue. Sancho Panza, his erstwhile sidekick has given up trying to convince the senile old man that he's on a fool's journey and tries to protect him as best he can. From place to place, the star of the show looks through the mists of madness and sees love and kindness, where others only see hatred and greed. His family and friends succumb to this loving lunacy at his death and their eyes are opened to the beauty and promise of life. Don Quixote's faithfulness to his quest and willingness to suffer deeply for it is the most moving subplot of the whole drama. Nothing can sway the "knight of the noble countenance" from serving God and his fellows with all of his vigor and devotion. If we had a generation of men with Quixote's perseverance, we could change the world.

So, why do we quit? Perhaps we're lazy, or afraid of hard work. It could be that no one ever taught us that there is value in diligence, or maybe we've convinced ourselves of the folly that the get-more-for-less mentality produces, so why bother ourselves? As with most things in our lives though, our indifference actually stems from a vision problem. If we believe that all that matters are the whims of the moment, we are not likely to expend a quark of energy to see the larger picture. In this context, my marriage is hardly worth the effort, since I can always find another wife more to my liking. And my children? They'll be grown before long, so they won't be a problem for much longer.

Surrendering to the current of expediency makes us slaves of our desires. When craving goes, so does our reason for living in that moment. Our world needs us to be men of commitment, persistence and vision. Glory awaits those who persevere, and ignominy trolls for the rest!

> *Do not grow slack in zeal, be fervent in spirit, serve the Lord.*
> Romans 12:11

Do you "cut and run" when the going gets tough?
Your children are watching and learning from you!

44

Envy Wounds and Gratitude Heals

*"When we cannot find contentment in our selves,
it is useless to seek it elsewhere."* Francois La Rochefoucauld

Picture a creek through which flows either crisp, clear water, or raw, contaminated sewage. The riverbed doesn't have much say about the content of the current: refreshing water trickles and sludge oozes down its length without permission. One life giving and refreshing, the other devastating and poisonous...the riverbed is only the channel along which blessing or debris flows. Our soul is like a river which floods with nourishing streams of gratitude or malignant cascades of envy and processes, without question, whatever we pour into it. William James noted that the greatest gift of our generation is the recognition that we choose how we will think about life. So, we are the ones who determine what floods the waterway of our lives. If we adopt gratitude as a companion in life, we sanctify our soul. But if we embrace envy, we flood our consciousness with a force so toxic that we lose the ability to love ourselves or anyone else.

Gratitude, the joyful recognition of the gifts I've been given is contrasted by envy, the realization that I want whatever it is that you have.

Such grasping need not be material. I may be so inadequate in my soul that I become envious at your success or good fortune. And that diminishes my soul as surely as if I wanted your plane, train or automobile. Envy has been with us since the beginning of human memory. Early on, Cain became a poster boy of the deadly effects of craving, but sadly the spirit of covetousness didn't die with him. Kingdoms have been toppled, families destroyed, cultures wiped out and beauty defaced by those who have drunk deeply of envy's elixir. St. Paul called this disorder, the "lust of the eyes" and St. James noted that envy poisons us with rancor, animosity, despair and the need to injure others to get what we want.

Our culture expects us to be envious and hundreds of millions of advertising dollars are spent to reinforce this social neurosis. Much advertising is an attempt to convince us that by getting the gadget, hair transplant, or hotrod that everyone else has, we will be happy. Not only is this assumption a lie, because happiness isn't a matter of acquisition, it is a recipe for personal and social disaster. We aren't the only victims of our envy; it wounds the membrane of society because it reduces us to people who own things that others want. Not so politely put, the enmity of envy has created neighborhoods that we can't safely walk in and people that we can't freely trust.

Our journey on the sacred path demands that we recognize our tendency to fill the emptiness of our hearts with envy and to replace it with the unction of gratitude. Since gratitude is the recognition that I have been given many good gifts, it puts me in a proper relationship with the Universe. Since a grateful heart recognizes gifts received as blessings from another, we are freed from the illusion that we "do it all." Gratitude also liberates my heart from the need of "more" and frees me to live in the here-and-now with peace of mind and joy. When one is grateful, our capacity to receive good things increases and drowns out the petty sorrows of life. As Gary Fenchuk reminds us, there are over one billion people on the earth who would trade places with you this very minute! So today, instead of lacing our hearts with envy and malice, and wondering why we're miserable, let's adopt an "attitude of gratitude" and see how the world softens in front of us.

For everything created by God is good and nothing is to be rejected if it is received with gratitude.
1 Timothy 4:4

> "What do I have to be grateful for?" you ask.
> Did you wake up in a bed this morning? Do you have a job?
> There are those around you who don't!

45

Suffering and Weakness? Great Teachers

*"God allows us to experience the low points of life in order to teach us lessons
we could not learn in any other way." C.S. Lewis*

A quick look at our prevailing masculine mythology will reveal two
things: men must avoid the appearance of weakness at all costs and suffer in stoic silence. As we've said before, a "real man" is a tough man, one
who laughs in the face of danger and leaps into battle with the ferocity
of a Visigoth. Look at the hero-worship of the modern athlete and
mega-tycoon for examples of men we esteem. We admire the quarter-
back who takes eighteen pain injections so he can keep on playing and
are in awe of the man who works himself to death, if he strikes it rich,
that is. I do not disdain perseverance, commitment and courage, since
we've praised those virtues in this book. But for too many men, the fear
of weakness and dependence on others is pervasive and deadly. Men are
willing to sacrifice physical and mental health, family harmony and
spiritual insight to remain quarantined in a shell of self-protection.

Yet, the message of the Gospel is that strength is discovered hiding in
weakness and healing is concealed deep within suffering. While this
would not be the spiritual inclination of our age of affluence, it is at the

root of Jesus' view of the authentic life. His way of looking at the world has always seemed a little topsy-turvy, a bit off center, at least from our point of view. We want power and Jesus calls us to surrender, we opt for wealth and he points us to poverty. We run from suffering and weakness while the Son of God invites us to embrace the deepest things that we fear. In spite of Jesus promise that the results of such an embrace are peace of mind and joy, we'd just as soon pass, thank you very much. After all, who in their right mind wants to suffer? And what man wants to depend on another in his moments of embarrassment and weakness?

Perhaps the greatest value to suffering and weakness is that it forces us to acknowledge that in the thick and thin of life, we aren't God. In other words, our trials and shortcomings cause the reflective person to ask questions of sufficiency and confidence. Just who is it that we ultimately depend with the direction of our lives? In this age of "success in ten easy steps," the almost natural answer is, ourselves, of course. Trusting in God in this scientific and technological age seems a rather childish notion, quite like a nostalgic memory or prayer. And given the wonder of intelligence, virtue, talent and courage we possess, it's easy to forget that we are but a reflected glory. Like the beauty of the sun that emanates from the moon, we often think that our greatness comes from our own efforts. That is, until the walls of our lives come crashing down around us.

Then, as the twelve-step movements remind us, a spirit of humility whispers gently in our ears, reminding us that there is another way to live. It says that in the moments of our greatest need and vulnerability, we stand at the precipice of our greatest glory. Because nothing works as well as failure and suffering to show us the necessity for God and others. By surrendering our ego, new possibilities for life and love emerge. It's this type of wisdom that says that nervous breakdowns have been highly underrated as a tool for growth in holiness. As long as we still have recourse to our old ways of thinking, we will remain trapped in the mire of despair. But when we allow God to use our suffering to give us new sight, then the renewal of our life begins in earnest. For that, we can give thanks.

"I am content with weakness, for Christ's sake, for when I am 1 weak,
then I am strong."
II Corinthians 12:10

> Where do you feel trapped and in despair?
> It could be that God waits for you to have the courage to join him there on a journey, which will bring you a new life.

46

Make Goodness Your Goal

"Do the right thing every time. It will gratify a few and amaze the rest."
Mark Twain

I teach a workshop for religious professionals on ways to reach out to members of "Generation X," those young people now in their early 20's. Sometimes it seems like the Church speaks in a language that misses the mark with an experientially based generation like "X." Serious thinkers of this era point out the disconnection between the dogma of the Church and the lived experience of its members. They say that while we talk a good game about the life changing implications of a spiritual path, there's not much evidence of it in the lives of religious people they know. Instead of seeing faith communities that live out of an ethic of love, respect and service, their experience is one of dogmatic infighting, rejection and marginalization. This doesn't resonate deeply with an earnest young seeker.

Now it might be that a generation of people who've grown up in an entertainment age expects too much from institutional religion, but their yearning for spiritual experience is genuine. The Christian tradition has held from the beginning that the deepest need of the human heart is to have a personal, intimate relationship with the living God. Next is our desire to be grafted into what scripture scholars call the "Community of the Beloved," that is, a place where we find support, nourishment and challenge to navigate the corridors of our lives. So we can understand the anguish of the heartfelt inquirer who looks at the dissonance between the words of our mouths and the actions of our hearts.

Since spirituality is, as we've said before, a path of integration and healing, our call as people of faith is to live out what we profess. If we are Christian, then we've identified ourselves as men who have consciously chosen to live as Jesus lived and love as God loves: unconditionally and without restraint. The practical effect of this is that every time we act, we do so according to the principles of justice, mercy and goodness. We don't take short cuts around complex moral issues, we don't cheat, we don't lie, and we keep our promises and always try to help others.

This seems at once rather elementary and a bit easier said than done, but our generation of men would be well served to decide to do the right thing, every time. Compromise, duplicity and artifice are rapidly becoming tools of moral convenience by too many in our culture. The shadow side of special interest politics preaches a doctrine of ends-justifying-means to ensure victory over enemies and the virtue of perseverance is distorted by the "whatever it takes" mentality of business one upmanship.

To be remembered as a man took the call to love seriously means that we will leave a legacy of faithfulness and integrity in our wake. While deeply satisfying to the soul, the call to gospel faithfulness requires a measure of courage and resolve that seemingly few are willing to discover. Yet, the great men of history are those who planted gardens of righteousness and withstood temptations of expediency. The flowering beauty of their efforts invites us to drink deeply from the chalice of devotion so that we might become icons of faithfulness as well.

"You have been told, O man, what is good, and what the LORD requires of you:
Only to do right and to love goodness, and to walk humbly with your God."
Micah 6:8

Where do your actions betray the commitment of your heart?
If tabloid newspapers were to rummage around in your closets, would they find a man of principle or a man of appetite and expedience?

47

You Need Your Brothers

"Brotherhood is the very price and condition of man's survival." Carlos Romulo

One of the most consistent complaints of men who take spirituality seriously is that they are lonely. In our culture, men are encouraged to plunge wholeheartedly into the quest for power, prestige and possessions, so little attention is given to a spiritual life which might call all of that into question. Men are focused, by in large, on making it in the *real* world, so spirituality is seen as an adjunct to life, a helpful tool to make it through the day *if you need it*. Accordingly, any serious search for a path to God is viewed with a disdainful eye. After all, if it doesn't pay the bills or help me have some fun, why bother? As a result, finding men who want to talk about faith, prayer, relationships and justice can be a daunting exercise.

The phenomenon of masculine isolation begins long before we're thrashing about on the adult stage. Boys are taught to become competitive from their earliest days on the playground and rugged individualism is held up as their cultural ideal. "Big boys don't cry," "don't be a sissy," and "what doesn't kill you makes you stronger" are drilled into young men early on. Many men lament the fact that their fathers pushed them to grow up, to ignore pain and to become independent before they were ready. This parental shortsightedness leaves a wounding imprint on the young man's psyche. In his work on men and addictions, Jed Diamond lists the four shame-based core beliefs that men carry about as a result of too-early isolation.[14]

- I am damaged and therefore bad inside.
- To know me is to abuse or abandon me.
- If I have to rely on people to meet my needs, I will die.
- I must fill the emptiness inside me with more things (drugs, sex, alcohol, money, etc.)

These core beliefs are the legacy of the abandonment of our young men by their elders. Without a solid basis of love and understanding in childhood, boys grow up feeling fundamentally flawed. And in addition to the hole that this creates in men's souls, this toxicity is repetitive. In other words, unless we break the cycle of what was done to us, we will pass the same horror onto our children as well. Sadly, the Church has not always been quick to recognize the profound pastoral needs in its midst. So men, aching for community and a place to heal, turn elsewhere. Twelve-step programs and therapy groups have filled a void in our culture by providing a place for men to gather and share their lives.

The spirit of sacred masculinity is not lost to our time though. Men's groups are springing up because of the growing awareness that men are fundamentally spiritual and need a place to foster that journey. Struggling to remain faithful to the call of the gospel is impossible if it is a solitary exercise. It is a rare man who can bear the encumbrances of life without the support of others. Perhaps this is because by design, we were created by a God whose essence is community. The mystery of the Trinity points to a profound truth: ours is not an isolated God who reigns alone on a distant mountain. Instead, Christianity tells us that God is a mutual relationship of sharing between Father, Son and Holy Spirit. So, to live the God-life means that we have intimate, loving relationships: terrifying to most of us! Without the companionship of other men, we lack the necessary support to encounter life and thrive. Our glory as sacred men is diminished when we walk alone and our wounds lay in wait to be passed on to the next generation.

"How good it is for brothers to dwell together in unity!"
Psalm 133:2

> **Do you have the healing support of other men?**
> **If not, your soul is in danger.**

48

You Are Only Responsible for Your Own Feelings

"For the great benefits of our being—we look to ourselves." Seneca

One day, in the netherworld, Screwtape called his most trusted lieutenants together for a strategy session. He'd recently received an assignment from the Devil himself to find a way to torment twentieth century and he wanted the counsel of his aides. "Let us begin," Screwtape intoned with a seriousness befitting the moment. "The Prince of Darkness has ordered me to find a way to torture men's hearts and rob them of their peace of mind. Any suggestions?" Cautiously, a demon new to the infernal planning team, but very ambitious threw out, "Let's find a way to convince men that they only way that they'll ever be happy is by having more money than they can ever spend!" "Hmmmm," Screwtape nodded, listening intently. "Go on," he prodded the novice tormentor. "Well, everybody here knows that wealth never really makes a man happy. So all we have to do is convince him that the momentary rush he feels from acquiring wealth is the answer to all his problems, and voila…he's hooked!"

151

Beaming with pride, the goblin sat back in his chair and Screwtape looked around the table. "Next?" he asked, "We've got to give the man downstairs more than just one option." "I know," volunteered another, "let's trick men into thinking that what really matters is cosmetic appearance." Sensing that the others were baffled, he continued, "it's simple really. If a man thinks that he's only valuable when he looks good, he'll spend all his time, energy and money making sure that he has the perfect body!" "Yeah, yeah" another chimed in, "th s will be great, since there is no such thing as the perfect body, it'll drive them crazy! They'll be jealous, anxious, depressed and, dare I say it aloud, maybe even suicidal." The cheers from the table so startled the infernal gatekeepers that they called down to make sure everything was as it should be. Stroking his charred and sooted beard, Screwtape mused, "We're onto something here. We can make plastic surgery available for men to enlarge some parts of their bodies, reduce others and then watch them go mad when gravity takes its course."

Glancing around, the Arch-demon looked at an earnest goblin, who had been heretofore, mute and asked, "Well, Neurosis, you've been awfully quiet. What do you have to so for yourself?" With steely determination, "Dr. N.," as he was affectionately called in these parts said, "I think we're heading in the right direction. While this is not the first generation of men who are so stupid as to believe that power, prestige and possessions will make them happy, they seem to pursue the amenities of life with unfettered passion." "I think though," he said in a professorial tone, "that eventually they'll wise up, so I have a better idea. Let's exhaust all of our resources to convince men that other people's feelings are their responsibility and vice-versa." Looking at the uncomprehending faces of his audience, he explained, "Here's the thing. *We know* that no one can make someone else feel a certain way; because people believe and feel the way they've trained themselves to. But, if we per-suade men that just the opposite is true, that *they* are responsible for everyone else's feelings, this will make them miserable and drive them to an early grave!" In awe and silence, Screwtape and his lackeys all bowed with reverence to the new Master of hell.

Cry for discernment and lift your voice to heaven for understanding"
Proverbs 2:3

Who's emotions and feelings enslave you?
Who taught you that you have to make people feel one way or the other?

49

To Change the World, First Change Yourself

*"The world of those who are happy is different
from the world of those who are not." Ludwig Wittgenstein*

Today is Election Day in the United States. Across the country people are going to the voting booth in greater or lesser numbers to elect representatives and to pass or reject ballot propositions. As one who voted this morning, I strongly support the value of politics if it is understood within its proper context. The political process can help people define a shared vision of how to live in our common communities. It provides directions for governmental process and reinforces principles by which we are governed. Having said this, however, it's important to remember that in the end, politics cannot accomplish the most important change in the world: the conversion of the human heart. No referendum on people, places or things can dispel prejudice, ease hatred or change the way that we relate toward others.

Remember, an underlying principle of the spiritual life is that conversion of heart is an inside-out process. Grace visits us with occasions of transformation, but the choice to respond is ours. The invitation to embrace love, hope, courage and compassion comes to us daily and we

154

decide whether we will accept or deny their offering. So our decision to grow in grace or bury ourselves deeper in prejudice and fear is reflected in the way we relate to others. Laws may regulate my behavior in the moment, but the fact that we need law proves the point, until the human heart changes, the outer world will not affect the inner much.

While this seems self-evident in the world of politics, it's not too far off the mark in our personal lives as well. We often think that our world will be a much better place for us to live in if someone else behaves or thinks differently than they currently do. It's a human tendency to blame the outer world for the discomfort of the inner world. In other words, instead of changing the way I relate to the circumstances of my life, I would rather denounce you for my discontent. This inclination is singularly pernicious because it gives us permission, both personally and corporately, to label those whom we disagree with as enemy and work for their downfall. Again, just watch politics as usual. We believe that the problem with our City, State or Country is always "them." And since "we" are righteous and "they" are not, we feel morally justified attacking both them and their ideas.

This attitude wears on our soul as well because it denies us the opportunity to take responsibility for our lives. If I think that the outer world is liable for my comfort or discomfort, then I will spend all my energy trying to force *it* to change and never develop an ounce of understanding or compassion. The path of mature spirituality is to recognize that how I relate to the world is just that: my relationship to reality. If I think that people of a particular race, religion, social class or ideology are evil, then I automatically find ways to reinforce that belief at every turn. Likewise, if I have surrendered to loving overtures of grace and begin to see that peace of mind depends on my conversion, not another's, then I won't ask them to give what they can't. Only when authenticity is woven throughout our soul can the real work for peace and justice begin. For then we can find common ground with others and build something that will last as a testament to goodness for years to come.

"Watch over your heart with all diligence,
for from it flows the springs of life." Proverbs 4:23

Do I ask more of others than they can give?
Who tricked me into believing that others can give me peace of mind?

50

Immerse Yourself in Wisdom

"Our life always expresses the result of our dominant thoughts." Kierkegaard

Have you ever been accused of doing something of which you were absolutely innocent? I once lived through an experience where, despite my best efforts, every action and comment was misinterpreted by someone who tried to make life miserable for me. It was a horrible experience and before long I recognized that I was becoming depressed. Anger was laced with self-pity and it felt like every bit of energy was draining from me. As often happens with depression, I started to close myself off from friends who could comfort me in the injustice of the whole affair. Like Job, I took perverse comfort in sitting on the ash heap of wounded pride and I picked at my broken heart with potsherds of despair and self-hatred.

About two weeks into my emotional malaise, I ran across a copy of the Scriptures that I hadn't seen for a while. It was an older bible, one that I had taught from years ago and it was chock full of highlighted texts and hand scribbled notes. As I reread familiar passages, I absorbed the hope that had been laying in wait for me. Within a few hours, I discovered as St.

Augustine had before me, that bathing my mind in wisdom lightened my spirit and gave me a fresh perspective on my predicament. I realized that I had been taking responsibility for someone else's problems and try as I might, that I couldn't change their opinion of me. Understanding this helped me pick myself up and move on with life.

In this do-it-yourself world of self-sufficiency we forget that others have already struggled with the issues we face today: pain, sadness, anxiety and fear are the lot of the human race. People have suffered profound losses, made great gains and in the mist of all of it, found meaning and purpose for their lives. So we don't have to reinvent the proverbial wheel as we grapple with the struggles and challenges of life. We have the writings of men and women who've learned the lessons of the ages to bring warmth to our souls and clarity to our clouded vision.

Why do we fail to drink from the deep springs of wisdom that are available to us? Given the personal and societal darkness that confronts us, you'd think we would turn to every source of guidance that we can find. Instead, we take the easy way out and call Dr. Laura for a quick opinion on how to resolve the drama of our lives. Maybe we're too busy trying to make a living, commuting to work, coaching our kid's sports teams and catching an occasional movie to read anything that would challenge the way we think. Or perhaps we think that dusty old books have nothing relevant to say to our highly technological era. Worst of all, might it be that we hesitate to dig too deeply into sacred wisdom for fear of discovering an answer to our questions that we don't like?

Whatever our rationale, if we neglect the great thinkers of humanity we run the risk of a fuzzy mindedness which helps no one. While the advent of mind-body medicine amazes us, the spiritual masters have always known that the way we think dictates the course of our lives. Transformation of our thoughts leads to the transformation of actions.

Conversion has always been an act of rethinking, of seeing life in a new way…God's way. So our challenge as men of spirit is to embrace the sacred writings that point the way to life, meaning and joy.

"Do not be conformed to this world, but be transformed by the renewal of your mind."
Romans 12:2

Do you go to the Scriptures to learn something new or to reinforce your prejudices?
Have you read an inspirational book (besides this one) in the past year?

51

Don't Run From Life

"Mr. Duffy lived quite a distance from his body." James Joyce

One of the best-kept secrets of the spiritual life is that fear, not doubt is the opposite of faith. If faith is our ability to trust God in the midst of the unknowns of life, then it is a rare dogma that keeps us from plunging into the mystery of love. Rather, the chasm between head and heart is more often blocked by the apprehension of what is waiting just around the corner. One author suggests that the fear of the known is far more debilitating than the fear of the unknown. After all, it's the experience we've had in life that causes pain, sorrow and despair. So, whether the fear is of the known or unknown, it still erects an impenetrable barrier between us and our ability to trust God or anyone else. And when we live possessed by fear, we will do just about anything to avoid it.

Usually we try to diminish fear by fighting it, projecting it onto others, or trying to ignore it all together. None of these strategies works very successfully since they are all delaying tactics that force our terror into another disguise. As they say in Alcoholics Anonymous, "You can't stuff your feelings...nothing stays stuffed!" This doesn't stop us, though, from trying to find an escape hatch that we might slip away in. Eventually we will find a compulsive relationship to someone or something which takes our mind off our fear and replace it with momentary doses of synthetic calm. These are called addictions and they have slashed our culture to shreds.

We once thought addicts were derelicts or criminals who lurked in partially lighted back alleys. The reality is far more sobering. Some psychologists suggest that everyone is addicted to something and one theologian even goes so far as to say that the addictive process is the only proof we need for the doctrine of original sin. Those who work in the recovery field identify three types of addictions: substance, relationship or process. In other words, we can be addicted to things, activities or people. Jed Diamond, an expert on addictions writes that men are addicted to "food, marijuana, cocaine, alcohol, money, work, Valium, gambling, television, heroin, caffeine, sex, religion, nicotine and adrenaline"[15] with a frequency that is astounding. Men regularly also become addicted to fear, excitement, rage, the adulation of others, physical exercise and success.

Regardless of the type of addiction, they are all evidence of our ruptured connection to our spiritual life and us. Martin Buber reminded us that *spiritus* was originally translated from Latin as *an ability to breathe*. What a picture of well being this paints! When we are in a proper relationship to Spirit, we can breathe deeply and freely in all the circumstances of our lives. Compare this to the enslaving quality of the addictive process, because in the end, an addiction is *something that we are not free not to do*.

The journey to freedom leads us to wholeheartedly embrace life, God and ourselves. One writer calls recovery from addictions the "journey home." For it is only when we are inspired to integrate every part of our being, with all of our complexity and paradox, that the fingers of fear loosen their grip on our heart. It's true that life is messy and that life is *not* fair, but when we face life with honesty and the fellowship of our brothers, we can make it. We will laugh and weep, dance and tremble, celebrate and mourn, but we will be full of faith, complete, holy, and alive.

"The Lord will be with you and never fail you or forsake you.
So do not fear or be dismayed."
Deuteronomy 31:8

Tell the truth: Where are you hooked?
Who do you know who will support your quest for freedom?

52

The Question is not Who you are, but Whose.

"He who lives only for himself is truly dead to others." Publilius Syrus

Mahatma Gandhi was on a train tour of India and he stopped at a village to speak with the people there. After his talk was concluded, he boarded a train and began to study his notes for the next stop. Before the train started down the track, however, a young reporter ran up to the window next to where Gandhi sat and cried out, "Mahatma G! Please give me a message that I can take back to my people." Looking around for something to write on, Gandhi spied a tattered brown paper sack lying in the aisle. As the train inched forward, he wrote something onto the back of the bag and quickly threw it out the window to the zealous reporter now running alongside him. The young man stopped and picked up the bag only to discover the words, "My life is my message" inscribed there.

People like Gandhi change the world because they understand the necessity of a wholly integrated life. Most of us aspire to some degree of goodness, but it seems that life just gets in the way. To be successful in the corporate or political world we are tempted to yield to expediency and groupthink instead of living out of our core values. The luminous ones of humanity don't preach from one set of precepts and then live by another. Instead they live with such integrity and devotion that it seems as if they become inseparable from the message they proclaim. For them virtues of compassion, faithfulness, honor, discipline and patience are so woven throughout their personality that they stand in bold relief to the facade of shallow celebrity which afflicts so many of us.

Ultimately the way we conduct our affairs will rest in large part on who we believe that we are. If our primary allegiance is to our selves, political parties, social and economic class or family, then our lives will demonstrate that. Jesus knew this ages ago when he showed us that to discover one values all we need to do is follow their money trail. According to Jesus, what we deem important will be reflected by the way we invest the precious commodities of our life. That's why our experiences are our greatest teachers, because they show us what we really believe to be true and valuable.

John Wimber, the founding Pastor of the Vineyard Christian Fellowships once commented that, as Christian men, we should be known for what God is known for. In other words, if we have identified ourselves as one who has embraced Jesus, then we should live in a way that integrates his values in our lives. This is where we run into problems though. Even a cursory review of Jesus' teachings reveals a God who loves wholeheartedly, forgives continuously, and offers his life to anyone who would have it. Ours is the God of the underdog, the one who blesses the poor in spirit, the humble, the meek and the servant. The God of Jesus suffers with the downtrodden, celebrates with those who rejoice and offers the Kingdom of Heaven to everyone who is interested, despite their past. This doesn't fit too well with the success, status and sensuality of our age.

Yet, this is our way of life if we choose to be Gospel men. We walk a path of service where we seek the welfare of others as we would our own and give from the overflowing storehouse of our resources to strengthen and heal God's people. The world waits in the wings for you to become the saint that God created you to be. Let's get on with it!

"Let us not love with word or tongue, but in deed and truth."
1 John 3: 18

As the old question asks…if you were put on trial for being a Christian today, would there be enough evidence to convict you?

Some Concluding Thoughts...

As I pen these last few words, I sit with the dawn of a new morning in the Chapel of the Sisters of Mercy in Burlingame, California. Except for the penlight that illuminates my page, the chapel is still shrouded in darkness. The flickering light of the tabernacle candle and the tentative gleams of sun light streaming through stained glass reminds me that light, not darkness is my final destiny today. In front of me is a larger than life reproduction of Andrew Rublev's icon, "The Holy Trinity." Each of the three angels in the icon looks adoringly at the other and they seem poised to drink from the table's common cup. A closer look reveals no fear, no competition, no striving and no illusion. They are present to themselves and to each other with a holy radiance in a setting of love and fellowship. Those who know the icon's history say it is a powerful portrait of God's desire for humankind: love, mutuality, holy desire and friendship.

My hope, in writing this book is to encourage you to look deeply within your own heart to see how fit you are for love. The old catechism taught us that our purpose for being here is to love God and serve him forever. And the Christian tradition says that we most fully and authentically love God when we love each other with a wholehearted passion. Of course, the pathways to this love are sometimes rocky in the early part of the journey. We have been fed a poisonous pedagogy of self-centeredness, incomplete sensuality, domination and violence. All of this is rooted in fear, so we recoil when we should embrace, and we reject when we should invite. We run from love in a million different ways that keep us safe, but miserable.

God has given us an enormous capacity to love and our challenge is to grow into that luminescence every day of our lives. To do this though, means that we must grapple with the lessons that life presents us, which I hope to have communicated in this book. Consciousness, integrity, passion, glory, dedication, prayer, service, growth and vulnerability are the evidence of a life on its way to love. To be a loving man means that we must risk the pains and losses that vulnerability requires of us. But it is only when we break open the seals of our heart that we finally find the place and courage within to love.

God outfits us for this holy pilgrimage with a Sacred Vision which clears away the mists of fear and pain and shows us a way to live which brings fulfillment and joy. As the light of love streams, however tentatively, into the darkened chapel of our own hearts we being to see loving beings all around us. As the flame of love begins to blaze in our hearts, we *understand*, we *see* and we *know* for the first time. We realize, under love's tutelage, why it's important to care for the earth, protect the weak, worship the holy and give with abandon. When we finally recognize that this really is God's world, then we understand why it is important to love it all. Because in our loving all of this we finally discover the God who never left us.

Our call as men is to be Icons of God's love to this world. To do this, we must join with other men and learn how to love again. The community of men needs to become a safe place for us to get in touch with our grief, fear and loss. Deep grief is a constant companion and we need the support of our brothers to learn how to let it go. There is no way around this descent into our depths and pain if we are committed to a life of Christian discipleship. But when we finally surrender to love, *com-union* becomes real for the first time in our lives. Before his untimely death, Joseph Bernadin put it this way:

> "To live in the energy of the Incarnation is to know that real union with God, in the depth of our humanity, is not simply a hope or a wild dream, but a concrete possibility... The Incarnation means that nothing of our humanity is alien or untouched by divine power—birth, coming of age, rejection, triumph, friendship, betrayal, anxiety, bliss, the frightful darkness of death—all of our human experience becomes in principle a route of access to the divine."

Your life, with all of your hopes and dreams, disasters and joys is God's gift to you. But remember, your life isn't just about you. Everything that you do, as a man of spirit, has consequences for everyone in your life. So have the courage to surrender to a relationship with the living God and those brothers who will support you on your quest for holiness and purpose. We are called to be passionate men of a passionate God and only a fresh baptism of the Spirit of love will lead us into the life that we've only dreamed about. So live with passion. Build, create, dance, celebrate, give everything you've got to make this world a more loving place, but do it is as men of the light. Embrace the life and heart of Jesus which is God's daily offering as the way out of the murkiness of our secular age.

Please pray for me and I will hold you in my heart. Ours is a rich heritage, replete with glory, power and blessing. This heritage is your legacy, the legacy of Sacred Vision. If you pass on the gift of a vibrant and committed spirituality to your descendants, you will leave them with an inheritance wich endure unto the ends of the ages. As the Father has loved me, so do I love you.

David James
Motherhouse, Sisters of Mercy
Burlingame Regional Community

End Notes

1. M. Scott Peck, *The Road Less Traveled: A New Psychology of Love, Traditional Values and Spiritual Growth.* (New York: Simon & Schuster, 1978), p. 12.

2. Robert Johnson, *"Lying with the Heavenly Woman: Understanding and Integrating the Feminine Archetypes in Men's Lives."* (San Francisco: Harper San Francisco, 1994), p. 21.

3. Richard J. Foster, *Celebration of Discipline: The Path to Spiritual Growth,* (San Francisco: Harper & Row, 1988), p.24.

4. Cardinal Joseph Bernadin, *The Gift of Peace,* (Chicago: Loyola Press, 1997), p. 35.

5. Alan Jones, *Passion for Pilgrimage: Notes for the Journey Home,* (San Francisco: Harper San Francisco, 1989), p. 42.

6. Neal King and Martha McCaughey, Los Angeles Times, February 17, 1990, p. 76.

7. Richard Rohr & Joseph Martos, *The Wildman's Journey: Reflections on Male Spirituality,* (Cincinnati: St. Anthony Messenger Press, 1992), p. 78.

8. "We do not need to see with the Buddha's vision to understand karma. The same karmic laws he described act in our lives from moment to moment. We can see how death and birth take place each

day. Each day we are born into new circumstances and experiences as if it were a new life. In fact, this happens in each moment. We die every moment and we are reborn the next." Jack Kornfield, *A Path With Heart: A Guide Through the Perils and Promises of the Spiritual Life.* (New York: Bantam Books, 1993), p. 86.

9.   J.B. Phillips, *Your God is Too Small.* (New York: Collier/MacMillan Books, 1961), p. 108.

10.   Vina de Sola Pinto and Warren Roberts, *D.H. Lawrence: The Complete Poems,* (New York: Penguin Books, 1993), p. 114.

11.   David Knudsen, "Old Men, Muskrats and Adolescent Dreams," in *Crossroads: The Quest for Contemporary Rites of Passage,* edited by Louise Carus Mahdi, Nancy Gever Christopher and Michael Meade (Chicago: Open Court, 1996), p. 116.

12.   Sam Keen, *Fire in the Belly: On Being a Man.* (New York: Bantam Books, 1991), p 121.

13.   "But if a man says to his father or mother, anything of mine you might have been helped by is Corban, that is given to God." (Mark 7:11), p.125.

14.   Jed Diamond, *"The Warrior's Journey Home: Healing Men, Healing the Planet* (Oakland: New Harbinger Publications, 1994,), p.149.

15.   Ibid., p.161.

About the Author

The Rev. David C. James, Ph.D. is the Pastor of St. Mark's Episcopal Church in Tracy, California. He holds degrees in psychology, scripture and theology. A former Police Sergeant, Fr. David is a popular retreat speaker and conference leader. His previous work, "What Are They Saying About Masculine Spirituality?" (Paulist Press) was a contributor to the Christian men's movement.